YOU CAN'T
TAKE IT WiTH YOU

PROBATE, WiLLS, AND TRUSTS
EXPLAiNED BY STORiES

by Fred L. Vilbig

I.H.S. *Publishers*

Saint Louis, Missouri

Published by I.H.S. Publishers
St. Louis, Missouri
www.saintjosephradio.net

Cover and Illustrations: Eric Hirsch
Editor: Kelly Boutross
Interior Design: Trese Gloriod

Printed in the USA.

978-0-9847656-6-9

TABLE OF CONTENTS

PROLOGUE

THE REASON FOR THE BOOK

In my practice as an estate planning attorney, I talk to people almost every day about wills and trusts and probate. Having studied it in law school and practiced law for over 30 years, it is almost second nature. However, as I explain to my clients, that just isn't normal. Most normal people try to ignore the topic.

I've had a number of clients ask me if there is an easy-to-read book that explains all of this. I have to admit that I haven't found one. There are textbooks from law school. Even I find those hard to read. I did find some books that came close, but at 500+ pages, I doubted that any of my clients would read them. There are some shorter books, but they just didn't seem to be client-oriented. I didn't think they would be very helpful.

A year or so ago, in a conversation about marketing, one of our neighbors, Barb, suggested that I run an ad in a local suburban newspaper. We kicked the idea around, but just an ad didn't make much sense. However, Barb's idea stuck with me.

I started to think about the ad idea in the context of what I do all the time (you can ask my wife about this), telling stories. No one remembers a dry, academic discussion about a complicated topic. In my client meetings, to get a point across, I often tell a story. The story sticks with them, and the underlying idea tags along. So I started running a column based on these stories.

The response was very positive. People enjoyed the stories. People would walk up to me at the grocery store or at a restaurant and talk about something I had written. When I walk into a local coffee shop, Rachel, one of the baristas, often loudly tells me how much she enjoys some column I had written – loud enough for everyone in the restaurant to hear. When clients come in, they regularly mention the columns.

As time went on, when I would talk to clients, I would tell them that I had written a column on a certain topic. They would ask me to send it to them. Then I would have to find it. The columns were sort of distilled from articles on my blog at www.law-matters.net, but I did not have a good organization. So I would have to search through the blog articles to find the piece I wanted to send to the client. I realized that I needed to organize things. That's when I started putting this book together.

The book is organized centered around a story. I start with a brief overview of what estate planning is and then move into the first half of the story. Then I go a little more deeply into topics: lifetime issues; joint ownership and beneficiary designations; the probate process, including intestate succession (dying without a will, that is); a discussion of wills; a discussion of trusts; and then a group of special issues that just did not fit anywhere else. These include charitable planning, business planning, remarriage issues, etc. I wrap it up with the second half of the overall story. And then I added a postscript warning about Yogi Bear.

I do not by means of this book intend to tell you how to do your own estate planning. In fact, as you will see in the course of the book, I want to actively discourage that. It is not so much that I am trying to generate business as it is that I do not want you to leave a mess for your children. All I want to do in this book is to tell some stories to introduce you to some topics.

I hope you enjoy reading it.

INTRODUCTION

Before we really begin, I want to make some general comments about estate planning.

ESTATE PLANNING: WHAT IS IT?

From discussions that I've had with clients, it is pretty clear that most people at best have only a vague idea of what estate planning is. They've heard about wills and trusts, but they don't really know what they do. In some cases, they've heard horror stories about probate, but those stories may or may not be based on fact. Or they may have been through probate for a parent's estate and had a horrible experience. So the first question we need to address is: what are we talking about?

In America (at least for now), we have private property. Aside from taxes, claims, and lawsuits, no one can legally take your property from you. You have a right to hold onto or dispose of your property as you see fit, and you have the right to the income off of that property to the extent that it earns any.

The problems come up when you become incompetent or upon death. In either case, you are not capable of buying or selling property, depositing money or writing checks, investing money, signing contracts, or conducting any business at all. In effect, all of your assets are frozen.

In the case of incompetency, someone needs to take charge of you and your assets to make sure that you're taken care of. If you haven't created a power of attorney or a medical directive, the court can appoint a guardian of your person and a conservator of your estate. The guardian can make decisions regarding housing and health care. The conservator is responsible for the money. Typically, the guardian and the conservator are the same person, but not always.

In the case of death, all of the person's separate assets are frozen. When I was younger, I thought that was to protect the widows and orphans. I've since learned that it is just to make sure that your bills get paid. I was so naïve. As I'll explain later in the section on probate, the probate assets of a decedent are in a sense locked up for six months to allow the creditors to get a stab at the money, and once any claims are resolved, the remaining assets are freed up for distribution.

However, as we will discuss later in this book, not all assets are treated the same, depending on how they are held and the nature of the asset itself. For instance, during the life of a joint owner of a bank account, he or she can use some or all of the cash, but the joint owner of real estate or investments will be paralyzed without the consent of the other joint owners. In either case, the property passes to the surviving owner(s) on the death of the other joint owner. Pay-on-death ("POD") or transfer-on-death ("TOD") beneficiary designations let you avoid probate on death, but they afford no protection for incompetency.

As I suggested in the Prologue, it is not the purpose of this little book to explain all of the intricacies of estate planning. This is only a survey to help raise questions. It is not intended to, and will not, replace competent legal representation. However, I hope that it is a start for some people and maybe reinforcement for others.

I joke with clients when we meet that the door of the conference room has a force field that strips away everything we talk about in our meeting. In a way, that's true. The next day while driving down the street, clients typically wonder what it was that we talked about. Hopefully this book will help them to remember.

I think all of us learn best with stories. All the facts and figures bounce off our brains, but stories seem to stick with us; they resonate. This particular story is both true and false. It is true in that I have had clients experience one or more of the following incidents, but I've never had one client experience them all. However, I think that by telling this story, I set the stage for the discussion that follows. So this is the story of Jack and Judy.

THE JACK AND
JUDY STORY

Jack and Judy met in college. They dated for a while, fell in love, and got married. When they graduated from college, they both got good jobs and worked for a while. Then they got pregnant.

Judy had a little girl and named her Suzy. A few years later, they got pregnant again. This time they had a little boy and named him Bill. Then a few years later they got pregnant one more time. Judy had another little boy and named him George.

The kids grew up. They all played sports. Suzy danced. They were a happy family. From all appearances, they were a pretty normal family too. Bill and Suzy got married (not to each other) and had kids of their own. But sometime during college, something happened with George. Where he had been social and outgoing, he kind of retreated into himself. He started to stay in his dorm room and skip classes. Soon he had to drop out of college. He moved back home and stayed in his room. Most of the time, when Jack tried to talk to George about his future, George would just become angry. Soon, George and his parents reached a kind of détente where George lived his life, and Jack and Judy lived their lives, all under the same roof.

Jack and Judy grew older. People told them they needed to do some estate planning, but they really didn't think much about it. They even went to some dinner seminars. Jack just figured the kids would work it out when he was gone. Judy was too busy with the grandchildren to bother with wills or trusts. They did take the time to put some of their investments in joint names with their kids (which is a bad idea, as I discuss later), but that was all the planning they did.

As with all of us, Jack and Judy continued to get older. After some time, they realized they needed to move out of their home and into a retirement community with assisted living and nursing care options available when they needed them.

They found a very nice place, but they needed a large upfront deposit. They were going to use their investments for the deposit and then sell their house and use the proceeds from the sale of the house to pay rent and

other monthly fees. When they talked to their broker, she told them that the kids needed to agree to the sale of their investments since they had put those accounts in joint names. Jack protested, saying that these were his and Judy's assets, but the broker insisted. When they talked to the kids, Bill was fine with the sale, but Suzy decided it was a bad idea and refused to consent. Jack and Judy were forced to sell their house and use the proceeds to move into a less appealing retirement community. They figured that it was good enough.

Time passed. Jack and Judy moved into assisted living. Jack eventually needed nursing care, and he finally died. Judy developed dementia and became bedridden. Her health continued to decline. She ended up just being kept alive on machines since Jack and Judy had never executed living wills. A lot of their savings were eaten up with medical bills by being kept alive on machines.

Judy's condition continued to deteriorate, and the doctors knew that her time was near. They decided to call the family.

When Bill got the call, he was very distraught. He loved his mother, and wanted to see her before she died. With tears in his eyes, he rushed to the hospital. He didn't see the red light or the car speeding through the intersection. Bill lingered for a couple of days after the accident. In the

meantime, Judy died, and Bill then died soon afterwards.

With Bill gone, everything fell into Suzy's lap. George's condition had deteriorated. Suzy didn't want George to end up completely homeless, so she had him declared incompetent. She was appointed his guardian and had him admitted to Happy Acres, a group home.

When Judy passed away, Bill was still alive, so all of the joint assets had to be split three ways. Suzy got her share outright. George's share went into a custodianship account and was quickly taken by Happy Acres to pay for his care. Bill's share had to be probated. More on that in a minute.

In addition to the joint assets, Jack and Judy had life insurance and IRAs. Since they didn't do any planning, they never named beneficiaries. Those assets had to be probated, too.

Suzy opened a probate estate. She was quickly overwhelmed with paperwork. She had to hire an attorney (you can't do this on your own), petition to be appointed as personal representative, publish the notice of the estate, file an inventory, pay bills, file tax returns, and prepare accountings. It's a lot of work. During that time, since there was no will and George was not competent to consent to independent administration (discussed later), the probate process had to be supervised by the court. That means that the court had to approve just about everything Suzy did. During probate, the assets were pretty much frozen unless Suzy got a court order allowing her to spend some of the money. After a minimum of six months, she had to pay probate fees and prepare a proposal of distribution. Once approved, she could distribute the assets, close the estate, and be released from her responsibilities.

In the end, Suzy made out OK; she got her money. As with the joint assets, George's share went into a conservatorship account and was eaten up by Happy Acres.

Just like the joint assets, Bill's share had to be probated again. Since Bill was an apple that didn't fall far from the tree, he had no estate planning. Bill's wife had to go through all of the administrative hassle of a probate estate, just like Suzy had to do with her parents' estate.

But she didn't end up with everything. Bill's estate had to go through intestate succession. That's what happens when you die without a will. A portion of his estate ended up going to the minor children. Since the children were under 18, they couldn't even open a bank account. The kids' shares went into conservatorship accounts that can only be invested in CDs and government securities. A court order is needed to make any distributions.

This certainly wasn't what Jack and July really would have wanted.

What a terrible result!

What follows is a discussion of the legal issues involved in this case, told with some illustrative examples. At the end, I will come back to the story of Jack and Judy, so please stay tuned.

LIFETIME PLANNING

Before getting into a discussion of wills and trusts (the main thrust of this book), I want to take a few pages to talk about lifetime planning. As people in our society continue to grow older and older, disability planning becomes more and more important. We are seeing a rise in the instances of the various dementias just because people are staying alive longer. And I don't think this problem is going to go away.

POWER OF ATTORNEY ("POA")

When a person becomes incompetent, without anything further, no one has any authority to do anything with their property (assuming, of course, it's not in a trust, which we'll discuss later). It is frozen. The idea is that the assets are protected from thieves and predators. But then the bills don't get paid.

In order to avoid this situation without having to create a conservatorship (which I will also discuss later), we advise clients to execute a general power of attorney. With a power of attorney, a person can authorize someone else to handle their banking; take care of their insurance; make investments; run a business; buy, sell, or mortgage real estate; handle tax issues; and generally do all of the business that needs to be done.

A power of attorney is where you (as the "principal") authorize another person (as your "agent") to make specified decisions for you. When these were first developed in England (and then adopted in America), they had pretty limited utility.

The problem was that these powers of attorney were only good so long as the principal was competent to do whatever the agent was doing. However, anyone dealing with the agent really did not know if the principal was still incompetent. This had almost no value in estate planning, since when you most wanted these powers was when the principal was in fact incompetent.

Back in the 1980s or so, states passed what are called "durable" powers-of-attorney laws. These laws allowed people to appoint agents who can continue to act even when the principal becomes incompetent and in some circumstances even when he or she is dead. This made POAs very useful. However, to be durable, there must be specific language written into them. Without the "magic" language, they are not durable. It should be noted too that even if the POA is durable, some people or businesses may not accept them.

Another difference in POAs is that they can be immediate or springing. An immediate POA means that the agent can act right now. A springing power only gives the agent authority after a doctor (or more than one doctor) certifies that the principal is incompetent.

I recently met with a couple who came in to update their estate planning documents. They asked me to review their current documents which had been prepared by another attorney almost ten years earlier. What I found kind of surprised me.

In looking at their powers of attorney, the maker of the power had appointed his or her spouse as her or his attorney-in-fact. On the death or disability of the other spouse, the eldest daughter would become the attorney-in-fact. On the death of the eldest daughter, the youngest daughter would become the attorney-in-fact.

The problem was that these powers of attorney were immediate and not springing powers. As I mentioned, a springing power of attorney is not effective until a doctor certifies that you (the maker of the power) are incompetent. You retain complete control of your affairs until you really can't handle things. With an immediate power of attorney, you immediately give the agent the listed powers. Sometimes immediate POAs make sense, but that is more often the exception rather than the rule.

The powers of attorney that my clients had were not a problem as they sat across from me in our meeting. I had two competent, loving spouses facing me, both having full control of not only their own but also each other's assets.

The problem that I foresaw was what would happen when one of them became incompetent. When one of them became incompetent, then the powers he or she had over the competent spouse's property would then immediately pass to the oldest daughter. So what happened on the incompetency of one of the clients was the eldest daughter would gain control of the assets of the competent spouse. Although they trusted their daughter, they wanted complete control of their property for as long as they were competent. It was a strange result.

When I pointed this out to my clients, they were more than a little disturbed, which was understandable. It was not what they had been led to believe they were doing when they signed the documents several years earlier. Fortunately, we still had time to fix things.

It is important to note that although a principal is giving the agent in some cases almost unfettered power over their assets, this power is not unlimited. Agents acting under a power of attorney owe "fiduciary duties" to the principal. Fiduciary duties are a legal duty someone owes to a beneficiary under a trust or a principal under a power of attorney to act solely in the other party's interest. The trustee or agent is the fiduciary, and he or she is strictly prohibited from doing anything with the person or assets of the other person that is not in that person's best interest. What this means is that the fiduciary cannot pay his or her own bills with the other person's money and things of that sort. If there is a conflict between the beneficiary's or principal's interests and the fiduciary's interests, then the fiduciary must either act in the other party's best interest or resign. If the fiduciary breaches his or her duties, he or she can be sued and be liable for damages. This is serious business.

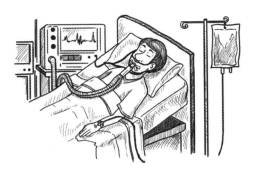

HEALTH CARE PLANNING

The other part of lifetime planning is planning for medical needs. Health care planning can be divided into two parts. The first part has to do with making medical decisions when you may be unconscious but will probably recover. These kinds of decisions have to do with admission to a hospital or rehab facility; surgery; medications; and other medical treatment. To make these decisions, someone has to see your medical records. Without written authorization, that won't happen.

These are the kinds of decisions that people normally make for themselves. However, when a person is incompetent, for one reason or another, someone needs to make these decisions. It used to be that family would have to go to court to have a guardian appointed to make these kinds of decisions, but once again, the state legislature has provided a solution.

To my knowledge, every state now allows these kinds of decisions to be made by an attorney-in-fact under a durable power of attorney. Although you could arguably wrap these powers into a general durable power of attorney, I think most attorneys have a separate health care power of attorney. Often, the best people to handle the finances are not the best people to make medical decisions. So there are usually two documents.

In a health care power of attorney, the principal can authorize the agent to agree to medical treatment; to take prescribed medicine; to agree to surgery; to be admitted to the hospital; to be admitted to a nursing home or rehab facility; or for any other medical treatment or procedure. You can also authorize your agent to see your medical records.

The second part of health care planning is the living will—this involves end of life decisions. This is where you tell everyone whether you want treatment to stay "alive" even though you are in a persistent vegetative state with no reasonable hope of recovering. This is when you are "brain dead," so to speak. If no treatment is going to improve your condition, do you really want CPR, radiation treatment, chemotherapy, or dialysis, just to name a few?

These end of life decisions are governed by what most states call a living will (some refer to it as an advance directive or medical directive). In a living will, you state what procedures you want withheld if death is imminent. These include artificial nutrition and hydration; any kind of surgical diagnostic procedure; CPR; chemotherapy; radiation therapy; dialysis; antibiotics; general surgery; and any other "life-prolonging" treatment or procedure that is not likely to substantially improve your condition. We also grant medical facilities permission to release the person to hospice care.

Usually clients choose to forego most of these treatments, but the one that has raised the most questions with faith-based clients is artificial nutrition and hydration. The moral question is whether the treatment is ordinary or extraordinary.

Many faith traditions (such as my own) believe that we are morally obligated to take advantage of ordinary means of sustaining our lives, but not extraordinary means. It's pretty certain that chemotherapy is extraordinary.

Artificial nutrition and hydration is another thing. In industrialized nations, it has become so commonplace that many consider it to be ordinary. The reasoning is (and I personally agree) that if it is ordinary, it would be immoral to forego that treatment. However, that is a decision everyone needs to thoughtfully make for himself and herself.

In talking about health care planning, I should say something about the Health Insurance Portability and Accessibility Act ("HIPAA"). The idea behind this law was to protect health insurance coverage for workers and families when they changed jobs. However, the biggest consequence that people see from the law is that doctors and hospitals won't talk to anyone about your situation unless they have written authorization. One of my former partners who actually read the law (it's several inches thick and really dull reading, by the way) said that this was an extreme overreaction to the actual language, but that's the way people are interpreting it.

Right after the law was passed, an attorney got a call from a hospital in Colorado where his 17-year old daughter was skiing. They told him that she had been in an accident, and he needed to go out there. When he asked what had happened, they said they could not tell him. When he asked why, they simply said, "HIPAA." Can you imagine that flight?

Doctors and hospitals have become more understanding in these matters, but it is still an issue. One of the things you can do with a health care power of attorney is to authorize health care providers to talk to your spouse or children or other family members.

The questions about health care planning are going to become more and more critical. In 1900, an average male (but then which one of us is really average?) had a life span of a little over 46 years. Women could expect to live until a little over 48. By 1950, men had a life expectancy of a little over 65, and women could expect to break 70. By the year 2000, life expectancies reached 74 for men and 79 for women. We are living longer.

However, longer lives bring other issues. The instances of dementia, whether simply senility or Alzheimer's, create problems. As we live longer, health care planning becomes more and more crucial for just about everyone.

In our story of Jack and Judy, you will remember that since they had not done any planning, Judy was kept alive on machines until most of their money was gone. I'm sure that's not what most (if any) people would want. A little planning would have helped a lot.

JOINT OWNERSHIP

JOINT OWNERSHIP

In our story of Jack and Judy, you will recall that they thought all they needed to do to plan their estate was to put their assets in joint names with their children. It did not turn out so well for them. Let's look a little more closely at joint ownership.

Joint ownership with right of survivorship seems so simple. During their lifetimes, two or more people own property together. When one of them dies, the survivor (or survivors) then owns the property outright. This seems like a simple way to get around probate, right? But nothing is ever really all that simple.

As I mentioned earlier, different rules apply to different types of joint property. Bank accounts, for instance, have special federal rules that apply to them. During the joint lives of the joint bank account owners, any one of the joint owners can do whatever they want with the bank account. They can even withdraw everything in an account without the knowledge, much less the consent, of the other joint owner. And that happens.

Other joint assets are much different. If you own a home or stocks jointly with another person, then neither of you can do anything with that asset without the consent of the other joint owner(s). In effect, unless all of the joint owners agree, one joint owner can veto what the other joint owners want to do.

Let me illustrate.

A CARING DAUGHTER

I got a call some time ago from a woman who was in tears. She was crying so hard I could barely understand her. When I finally got her to compose herself a little, the first thing I heard was "My daughter won't let me sell my house."

That, of course, raised a lot of issues in my mind, so I started asking questions. It turns out that a bank teller (typically a source of bad legal advice, by the way) had been talking to the mom. The mom had heard horror stories about probate, and the teller told her she could avoid probate by "putting her daughter's name on things." Assuming the teller was referring to a survivorship or a POD designation, that much is in fact true.

I understand why she said that, but it was bad advice. With any property other than bank accounts, as I mentioned, all joint owners must join in transactions affecting the joint property. So when the mother put her daughter's name on the house, she gave up control.

Time passed, and the mother aged. Now she needed to go into an assisted living facility. To do that she needed to sell her house, and her daughter was saying no. It was her inheritance, so why would she want to jeopardize that. Mom would have to make do.

I don't know how this situation got resolved. Did the daughter relent or did the mother have to stay in the house until she died? In any case, the moral of the story is that joint ownership can be a real problem.

THE UNFUNDED TRUST AND THE DEVOTED SON

In another case, I had a client come to me many years ago because her son had frozen her assets. She had been married for many years, but her first husband had died. They had done extensive estate planning, but they had skipped one step. They had never funded their trusts… at all. After her first husband died, in order to avoid probate, instead of funding the trust (which would have made sense to me), she put everything in joint names with one of her sons, who was actively involved in the family business. Things went along fine for some time.

However, over time, mom got lonely. She did what every 79-year-old widow does when looking for love. She ran an ad in an alternative newspaper (I can't make this stuff up). She met a guy 10 years younger than her.

He had been a CPA, and he was kind of gruff. If you talked to them for less than five minutes, you probably hated him. If you spent more time with them, you realized that he had a heart of gold.

The devoted son talked to him for less than five minutes and hated the boyfriend. He told his mother to dump the boyfriend, or he would "freeze all of her assets." Mom said, "No!" He froze the assets. He refused to consent to any sales or withdrawals of anything regarding the assets. Years of litigation ensued.

Post script: although 10 years younger, the boyfriend's health was bad. He'd have to catch his breath when he got to the top of the stairs. I convinced them to get married for tax reasons after working out a prenuptial agreement. But the new husband predeceased the mom. While driving the mom home from the funeral (her kids didn't even come), she said, "I don't regret it a bit. My years with [the new husband] were the happiest time of my life." The family never reconciled.

BUT WHAT ABOUT THE KIDS?

I'd like to share one other case that illustrates the dangers of joint ownership. Sylvia had been married for years to Dave, and they had four kids together. As happens many times, Dave predeceased Sylvia. Sylvia was fairly young, and over time, she got lonely.

Sylvia met Louie at a seniors' event at their church. Louie was also a widower. They enjoyed each other's company and started spending time together. They were sort of old-fashioned, so they ended up getting married. Not a bad thing really.

Sometime after that, Sylvia got sick. Louie nursed her all during her illness, but in the end, she died. Louie had loved Sylvia, and after losing his second wife, he was brokenhearted. He didn't live that much longer himself.

After Louie's funeral, Sylvia's kids started asking about their mother's estate, only to come to a rude awakening. You see, Sylvia and Dave had executed wills when their kids were younger, but they had never done anything else. After Dave's death, when Sylvia married Louie, she put her assets in joint names with him. This all seems very innocent.

The problem is that with joint property, on the death of the first joint owner, the assets belong entirely to the surviving joint owner. When Sylvia died, everything went over completely to Louie. Louie probably didn't have a plan, but even if he did, it certainly didn't take Sylvia's kids into account.

So when the dust settled, Dave and Sylvia's kids ended up with nothing. Louie's kids got a windfall. That's probably not what anyone really wanted, particularly not Dave and Sylvia's kids. A little planning would've gone a long way.

Although people hate to think about dying or spending money on an estate plan, joint ownership is not the solution. It usually ends in a mess. It simply is a bad idea.

BENEFICIARY
DESIGNATIONS

Now I want to talk about beneficiary designation, also known as "non-probate transfers." This is an option that Jack and Judy did not use since they thought that the joint ownership covered their bases. However, non-probate transfers are another possibility with pluses and minuses to them, so it is important to understand them.

NON-PROBATE TRANSFERS

As I discuss in more detail later, probate can be difficult and expensive. We've seen that joint ownership is not a good solution, but there is an alternative.

Many states have adopted some form of the nonprobate transfer law. You'll want to check your local laws to see if your state has done so. The nonprobate transfer procedure usually has three different forms that basically do the same thing with different categories of assets. "Pay-on-death" ("POD") clauses are used with regard to bank accounts. "Transfer-on-death" ("TOD") clauses are applicable to all other personal property, such as cars, boats, trailers, stocks, and bonds. Beneficiary deeds are used with regard to real estate.

With regard to these nonprobate transfer documents, they all basically work the same way. The owner designates a beneficiary in some sort of a "beneficiary designation." Unlike with joint property, these beneficiary designations do not affect title during the owner's lifetime. During his or her life, he or she can sell the asset, mortgage the asset, remove the beneficiary designation, or add more beneficiaries. These designations are only effective on the death of the owner, at which time the asset passes to the designated beneficiary without probate.

The success of these strategies, however, doesn't only depend on whether you do everything right in setting them up. You can "dot all of the i's" and "cross all of the t's", but still have problems.

We don't know what tomorrow will bring, much less what will happen 10 or 20 years from now. Your POD beneficiary might be fine today, but what happens if he or she has a stroke or dies? When those things happen, people often forget to change their plans. We seem to think that once we've done something, it's done. Out of sight, out of mind.

If a beneficiary is incompetent when the owner dies, then those assets can end up in a conservatorship. With regard to a deceased beneficiary, you can name alternative beneficiaries, but most people don't. If you just list your children as beneficiaries, on the death of one of the named beneficiaries, the other surviving named beneficiaries typically get the account or property.

The law does allow you to write creative beneficiary designations that can take future events into account, but this can be problematic. I do this kind of thing every day, but regular people don't. It's hard to think through all of the possibilities.

In addition, there are the bank rules. Banks don't want you to be too creative because it can get them into trouble. They typically only allow clear, straightforward, limited beneficiary designations on accounts. This doesn't allow for much planning.

It should be noted that non-probate transfers do not frustrate creditor claims. Creditors can still collect from these accounts any amounts owed by the decedent. One of the problems is that the creditors can go after one account but not any others. If the accounts are given to different beneficiaries, then one of the beneficiaries may bear all of the burden of unpaid debts.

These kinds of non-probate transfers can work in limited circumstances. However, it is my experience that those situations are few and far between. The best way to address the uncertainties of life in your estate plan is either through a will (although this guarantees probate) or through a trust.

Clients who try to do everything by themselves often leave their children in difficult straits. The kids may need to set up a conservatorship for a disabled beneficiary. If they predecease their parents, their share could go to their siblings and not their heirs. That's probably not what anyone wanted.

IRA PLANNING

With a retirement account such as an IRA or a 401(k) account (including the exempt organization version, the 403(b)), you can name your beneficiaries. Most people do name a beneficiary on these accounts. However, a lot of times they just name their spouse. If they do not name anyone or the spouse dies first and there is not a contingent beneficiary, just like in Jack and Judy's case, those amounts will have to go through probate.

IRAs and 401(k) plans are great. Amounts an employee contributes to them are tax-deductible up to certain limits. Amounts contributed to them by employers don't get included in taxable income when they're contributed.

And then the amounts in these accounts grow tax-deferred. Even though amounts withdrawn are taxable when taken out, the tax-deferred growth super-boosts the investment returns while the assets are sheltered in these accounts.

Once an account owner reaches the age of 70 ½ years, he or she must begin taking the "required minimum distribution" ("RMD"). You calculate this RMD by dividing the amount in your account by your life expectancy. It's kind of creepy, but the IRS has determined your life expectancy for you. That's so kind of our government, isn't it?

When you die, if you're married, your surviving spouse has the right to roll your IRA or 401(k) over into his or her own name. Assuming the surviving spouse is younger, then they can recalculate the RMD and extend the payments a little more. And all the while the money in the account continues to grow tax-deferred. Great benefit!

When I meet with couples, their biggest asset (or at least one of their biggest assets) is usually their retirement account. But the problem is that if the account owner doesn't plan carefully, on the death of the surviving spouse, some of the benefits can be wasted.

For instance, as in the case of Jack and Judy, I have had a number of estates where on the death of one of the spouses, the survivor rolled the IRA over to his or her name and failed to name a subsequent beneficiary of the retirement account. In that situation, the IRA is payable to the decedent's estate. When that happens, all the IRA assets must be distributed within five (5) years, and all of these distributions will be fully taxable. In addition, probate fees would be due. You can lose 45% of the account value in pretty short order. It seems a pity to waste all those lifetime tax savings that way, but people do it when they don't plan.

If people have a charitable inclination, a good plan is to have retirement assets payable to the charity. Although the retirement assets are income to the recipient, since a tax-exempt entity is, well, tax-exempt, no taxes are due.

If an IRA owner has children, a lot of people will just name the kids as the beneficiaries. This creates what is called an "inherited IRA" that can be stretched over the life of the recipient, which is a good thing.

But inherited IRAs can also be problematic. If the designated beneficiary dies before the IRA owner dies, then depending on the wording of the designation or the policies of the IRA administrator, the retirement assets may or may not go to the deceased beneficiary's children and the measuring life will probably be that of the deceased beneficiary.

Inherited IRAs also present another problem. One of the

laws that govern IRAs is the "Bankruptcy Abuse Prevention and Consumer Protection Act of 2005." (Where do they come up with these names?) Under that law, an employee's IRA is protected from bankruptcy. That much was pretty clear.

For several years after that, people wondered if the law also protected inherited IRAs. In the 2014 case of *Clark v. Rameker*, the Supreme Court decided that the law did not protect inherited IRAs from bankruptcy. If inherited IRAs are not exempt from bankruptcy, I wonder if they are protected from a beneficiary's other creditors at all. I haven't seen any cases on that, but it seems like a logical extension of the *Clark* case.

Another problem with an inherited IRA is that a young beneficiary (whether a child or a grandchild) would be able to withdraw the entire IRA principal at any time. When they do that, they will lose the tax deferral benefit. In addition, large sums in young hands often lead to ruin.

In order to protect against the poor judgement of youth, lawsuits, and bankruptcies, I tell clients to have their IRAs flow through a trust. By putting a trustee between the beneficiary and the IRA principal, it makes it hard for a young person to get their hands on the money for something they really don't need or that might even hurt them. In the case of litigation, although a judge can order the beneficiary to pay a judgement, the trustee is not a party to the lawsuit and has duties to multiple beneficiaries. Judges typically respect this distinction.

As I mentioned, the way to protect inherited IRAs from a beneficiary's creditors is to have the IRA paid to a trust. Now it can't be just any trust. If the IRA can be used to pay the debts of the decedent, trust, or probate administration expenses, court ordered family allowances, various taxes, or other things, then the trust is not qualified. If a trust fails to meet the requirements, then the taxes will be due within five (5) years.

In 1999, the IRS gave us some magic language to qualify a trust to receive IRA benefits. So in order for a trust to qualify, it must include this magic language. In addition, the trust needs to contain what's called a spendthrift clause. This simply says that the assets of the trust cannot be used to pay the debts of the beneficiary. If the trust satisfies the requirements, then the IRA assets can be paid out over the life expectancies of the designated beneficiaries, and taxes are paid over the lifetimes of the beneficiaries.

An IRA paid to a properly drafted trust will protect the inherited IRA from the beneficiary's creditors over the life expectancy of the beneficiary. It's a good plan.

As you can see, IRAs are great retirement planning devices, but are a little problematic for estate planning. However, with a little planning, an IRA can continue to grow tax-deferred and benefit your children for years to come.

PROBATE

If you remember, Jack and Judy's family had to deal with a couple of probate estates. When Jack died, everything went to Judy by joint ownership. When Judy died, the joint assets went to the joint owners, but some of the assets had to be probated. And when Bill died, all of his separately held assets had to be probated. We need to take a moment to talk about what probate means.

THE PROBATE PROCESS

When a person dies, any assets (whether real estate or bank accounts or investments or anything else) that are in his or her name alone will have to be probated. As mentioned earlier, joint property does not have to be probated. TOD and POD assets do not have to be probated because they pass automatically to the surviving designated beneficiary (if any). If you remembered to designate a beneficiary of your IRA or 401(k) account, that won't have to be probated, although if no beneficiary is named or living, even those assets have to be probated. And life insurance also escapes probate, so long as there is a living, designated beneficiary. Basically everything else has to be probated.

Although some people run screaming at the mention of probate, it's not really that bad. (Of course, this is coming from a probate lawyer.) It's just a very formal process. If there's a will, it has to be filed (sometimes within a limited period of time after the decedent's death – in Missouri, it is one year) with the probate court in order to be valid.

(Filing a decedent's will makes sense even if the family doesn't immediately know of any probatable assets.) As I will discuss later, in order to have a valid will, the signature of the testator (or testatrix in the case of a woman) must be witnessed. In Missouri, it requires two (2) witnesses. When a will is admitted to probate, there must be evidence that these signatures are valid. So either the witnesses have to be dragged into court to say, "Yep, that's my signature." Or when the will is signed, you have everyone's signatures notarized. The notarization proves it a valid signature. These later wills are called self-proving wills.

Once the probate estate is opened, notice of the opening of the estate has to be published in a local newspaper, and that starts the "claims period" (which in Missouri is normally six [6] months) running. A personal representative (or an executor/executrix) must be appointed. Typically within 30 days or so, an inventory of all of the decedent's property must be filed. It can take some time to sort through everything to make sure that all of the assets have been identified.

During the claims period, any creditors can file claims which a personal representative can allow or challenge. If challenged, there is a court hearing. While possible claims are being processed, unless the will includes a provision calling for a specific distribution of a non-cash asset, the personal representative should work with the other beneficiaries and sell any of the non-cash assets. Although a personal representative can always distribute those kinds of assets, cash is much easier.

At the end of the claims period, any unfiled claims are cut off. At that point, the personal representative must file an accounting and a proposed schedule of distribution. If everything is approved, the personal representative can distribute the probate assets and be relieved of his or her duties.

Although the duties of the personal representative would basically be the same, there are, in fact, two forms of probate administration. One is referred to as supervised administration, which is how Judy's estate had to be probated. Under this form, everything needs to be approved by the court, even the final accounting. One time I was 3¢ off on balancing a final accounting. I reached into my pocket to pull out the three cents. That was not the thing to do. It was not well received. It took us two weeks to find the three cents. My paralegal had transposed two numbers. Supervised administration is a lot more work for everyone.

The other form of probate administration is independent administration. That form can be selected in the will, or if it isn't, then all of the beneficiaries can consent to independent administration. Under this form of probate, court approval is required only when there is some kind of complaint or objection. As long as all of the beneficiaries are okay with what the personal representative is doing, the court doesn't need to get involved. It makes probate administration so much easier. In either case, though, probate is somewhat of an involved process that ends up costing quite a bit of money.

SMALL ESTATES

In the story of Jack and Judy we did not talk about this because their entire estate had to be probated, so it was a larger estate. However, even with well-planned estates, people miss things. Here's a relatively simple solution.

The poet Robert Burns once wrote a poem entitled, "To A Mouse." No one really remembers the poem, but it contains one of the most famous lines (or at least perhaps one of the most often quoted lines) of all poetry. In the original, it reads:

"The best laid schemes o' Mice an' Men

Gang aft agley ...."

We know it as, "The best laid plans of mice and men, oft go astray."

People may do their best to cover all their bases (or maybe not), but inevitably something is overlooked. A person may plan to get all of their assets into joint names, with a POD or TOD beneficiary designation, or into a trust, but they miss something. Usually it is something small, but it should not be ignored. So what to do?

As I discussed in the preceding section, probate can be kind of involved. So the legislature has authorized administration of a "small estate." Small, of course, is a relative term. Depending on the state, "small" can mean less than $40,000 as in Missouri or up to $100,000 in Illinois ($150,000 in California). Generally these are net amounts after subtracting liens, but check applicable state laws. Regardless of the amount, a qualified small estate can be administered much easier.

In Missouri (as in several other states), we in effect have 2 tiers of small estates. The first tier is sometimes referred to as a "creditor's refusal." (Refusal refers to the fact that the court refuses to open a full-blown probate estate by issuing letters of administration that authorize the personal representative to handle the estate.) This is for estates of less than $15,000 consisting of only personal property (no real estate) and where there is no surviving spouse or unmarried minor children. In these estates, no published notice is required (more on that in a minute). In order to process a creditor's refusal of letters, the creditor just has to file an affidavit with the probate court. As with any claim against an estate, the affidavit must be filed within one year of the date of the person's death, or it is void.

The second tier of small estates is sometimes referred to as a "spousal refusal," although a surviving spouse is not actually necessary. This is for all estates under $40,000 (or whatever the local maximum is) where a creditor's refusal does not apply. In Missouri, notice of the administration is required to be filed in a local newspaper for 2 consecutive weeks.

Notice is a somewhat technical requirement that varies depending on the legal proceeding involved. For regular lawsuits, it might involve a process server who hides in the bushes, waiting for the defendant to show up (actually they usually just sneak up on you). When you don't know who the other claimants might be or where you can find them, the law allows you to publish the notice in a newspaper of general circulation in the area where the legal action was filed. The idea is that you can't take something from somebody unless you give them a chance to state their case. Once the notice has been filed, the affidavit then has to sit at court for at least 30 days. At the end of this process, the court will sign off on the affidavit.

Some states (such as Illinois) do not even require court approval, which strikes me as kind of dangerous. You can take the affidavit to the bank or investment advisor, and the funds are released. If you're dealing with real estate, you can take the affidavit to the title company as proof of your right to sell.

Small estates can be an efficient way to deal with these smaller amounts that need to be administered.

DYING WITHOUT A WILL

Jack and Judy were not alone. A few years ago Forbes did a survey. They asked people if they had a will. They found that 51% of Americans age 55 to 64 do not have a will. They also found that 62% of people between the ages of 45 and 54 do not have a will. Some studies have found that 64% of the overall population does not have a will.

Even if we assume that some portion of the population may not need a will per se (elderly people on public assistance, for instance), a significant portion of the population does not have a will. Dying without a will is referred to as "dying intestate", and the estate will be distributed pursuant to the rules of "intestate succession."

From my perspective as an estate planning lawyer, that represents a significant risk to a large number of families, but I don't think people really understand what that risk is. So one of the questions people should be asking is, "What happens if I die without a will?"

As I tried to show in the Jack and Judy story, there are several different areas of concern. First, if you have young children, parents should be asking what will happen to them. If both parents die in an accident and there isn't a will, the court will appoint a guardian. Do you really want a court to decide who will raise your children?

When working with clients with small children, this is always one of the biggest questions they have to overcome. Who will take the children? By not having a will, the parents are just delegating that decision to a judge they don't know. The judge will usually look at family members, but he or she will probably look at objective measures such as financial stability in deciding, but that may not be the most important factor to parents. Your children could end up with successful relatives who don't have time to raise them.

One of the other problems with intestate succession is how the assets will be divided. As discussed earlier, joint property, of course, will go to the surviving joint owner. TOD and POD property (as discussed earlier) will go to the designated beneficiary. But with regard to your separate property, your state has written your will for you, and the survivors may not like it.

The rules of intestate succession vary from state to state, and I do not propose in this book to provide a survey of the various state laws. Instead, I will simply use Missouri as an example. Missouri has a version of the Uniform Probate Code (the "UPC") that has been adopted by several states, so this may not be far off from your own state's rule.

In Missouri, if a married person with minor children dies without a will, his or her separate property is distributed as follows: the first $20,000 goes to the surviving spouse, and the rest is split 50-50 between the surviving spouse and the surviving children. I assume that the reason the legislature did that was to make sure that the children got something, but I doubt that is how most people would plan their estate.

Another problem with intestate succession is how the decedent's property gets distributed. If an heir (one of the descendants) is under 18, his or her share goes into a conservatorship. The conservatorship usually can only invest the money in government insured bank accounts or treasury bills or notes, but typically those don't even keep up with inflation. The conservator can only spend money with court approval, so they will have to abide by a strict budget approved by the probate court. Everything has to be accounted for to the court. This process involves both time and expense, and the assets will be distributed pursuant to state law, and not pursuant to the decedent's wishes.

When an heir is 18, he or she will get their inheritance outright. I don't know about you, but if I had received a large sum of money when I was 18, I would've been reasonable and prudent in handling it. Oh wait! No, I wouldn't have. In fact, I might have developed some really bad habits until the money ran out. At least that's what I've seen young heirs do in my law practice. Many times the end result has been tragic.

So dying without a will typically is not a good plan. However, in another study conducted by Rocket Lawyer, they asked people why they didn't have a will. I would have assumed that the main reason was that people don't want to think about dying. That's kind of a depressing topic. I also would have assumed that people put off doing any estate planning because of the costs. However, that wasn't even in the top four reasons.

The denial of death came in at number four with only 14% of the people stating that was the reason that they had no will. The clear majority, 57%, simply said they hadn't gotten around to it. Coming in at number two with 22% were people saying that it wasn't an urgent issue for them.

Both of these seem to be one form or another of avoidance. So the basic reason people don't have wills is because of procrastination. I think that is a bad idea.

WILLS

In talking to clients about estate planning, I am often surprised by how little people know or understand about a will. There are several stories and movies where there is a "reading of the will" (I don't think that ever happens, by the way), but I guess people don't really understand the significance of the will to the story's plot.

WILL BASICS

The basic estate planning document is a will. In its most basic form, it is a set of instructions to your personal representative (or executor/executrix) about what to do with your property when you die.

Each state has a law usually referred to as a "statute of wills." It sets forth the requirements for a valid will. Although the laws of the various states vary, as I mentioned earlier, most states have adopted some version of the UPC (mentioned before). Since a discussion of the probate code of all 50 states would be a monumental task, I am again going to limit my comments to the laws of Missouri, which has adopted a version of the UPC. But if you are in a non-UPC state, these comments may not apply.

To be valid, the will must be in writing. It can be handwritten, but only in a very narrow circumstance. These are called "holographic" wills. Holographic wills are valid if at the time you write it you are in imminent fear of dying and actually die as a result of whatever it is that motivated you to write the holographic will. For instance, if you are a soldier going into battle in fear of dying, but you die before from an infection you contract from your unhealthy living conditions, the handwritten will you wrote the night before going into battle is probably not valid.

In order to execute a will, the person writing the will has to be competent. The required level of competency for writing a will is pretty low. The phrases we use are "sound mind and memory" or "disposing mind and memory." The person must have a general idea of the extent of his or her estate as to value and types of assets, but specifics are not generally required. The person also needs to know the "objects of his (or her) beneficence" (that's a good phrase from law school). In other words, the person making the will must know the people he or she would normally want to benefit, such as their family. You also need to be generally oriented as to time and place.

Your will has to be signed and witnessed by two disinterested witnesses. If the witnesses have an interest in the estate, they could end up being disinherited, depending upon how the will is written and administered. Their signatures don't have to be notarized, but as I explained in the section on probate, it helps.

Years ago I had a client show up with his brother's will. His brother had seen a friend's will and photocopied it. He whited-out the names on the will and wrote in his own kids' names and appointed his brother as executor. At the time, wills in Missouri needed three witnesses to be valid. He was a machinist, so he got a couple of his buddies at the shop to witness his signature. Apparently he couldn't find a third, so he witnessed his own signature. Fortunately, by the time he died, the law had changed so that you only needed two (2) witnesses. It was very irregular.

When I filed the will with the court, the judge called me in. He wanted to know where the original will was. I explained the situation and told him that he was holding the original will. He gave me one of those looks. He got out his magnifying glass and studied it very carefully. After quite some time and many more questions, he finally admitted the will to probate. I was relieved.

So what does a will do? In a will you indicate who should administer your estate, that is, your personal representative (or in some states, your executor). This is the person who is going to organize your stuff and take care of things. I wouldn't think who that person is would matter, but a number of my clients are very sensitive to who's going through their stuff, even after they're dead. Typically, the court will appoint whoever you name, although they don't have to. If the person is a convicted felon, the court will probably appoint someone else.

It is in the will where you designate who you want as guardian of your minor children. As I mentioned before, this is a big issue for families with small children. Once again, the court will typically appoint whoever you name, unless they are a child molester or something else that would make them wholly unfit for this role. If no one else is named, the court typically looks to the close family.

In your will, you also state how you want your property to be distributed. Later in the book, we will discuss this issue, which can get rather complicated.

As I discussed in the section dealing with probate, you'll want to authorize independent administration to simplify things. You have to do that in the will (or all the beneficiaries will have to agree to independent administration). If you want your personal representative to be able to sell your property, you need to give them the power to sell in the will. Otherwise, they'll need to get court approval to sell anything, and that's just an added burden.

The law requires that anyone serving as a personal representative must be bonded by an insurance company. That's an expensive proposition even if you can qualify. In your will, you can waive the bonding requirement.

WHEN IS A WILL THE (RIGHT) WAY?

I spend a lot of time talking to people about the benefits of trusts, which I discuss later in this book. The bottom line is that they avoid probate. In the chapter where I talk about probate, I discussed how probate can be slow, freezing cash and other accounts for a person, so that mortgage, utilities, and other necessary expenses can't be paid; probate is a public process that can open your private business for general inspection; and probate can be expensive (more on that in the section dealing with trusts). So why would anyone forgo a trust and only use a will?

There are a few instances when a will is the right way to go. Trusts cost a little more than wills, and for young families, a little added expense can be a large burden. In that case, a will would be far better than to ignore estate planning altogether.

If a young couple with children die without doing any planning, as I mentioned earlier, their children's lives will be caught up in the court system. First, there is the question of who will take care of the children. When working with couples with young children, this may be the most hotly debated (if not contested) issue. The wife never really liked or trusted the husband's brother, Billy, who is his best buddy. The husband never really thought much of the wife's sister, Lucy, to whom she is deeply devoted. Even so, I've never met a couple who wanted their children to become wards of the state and possibly bounced from foster home to foster home. By means of a will, they can name guardians for their children ... if they can agree on who to name.

In addition, couples don't really want their assets managed by the probate court or public administrator. With young families, these assets are typically life insurance proceeds, but they can be substantial. Young children cannot open a bank account; they cannot make investments; they can't even pay bills. Someone has to be put in charge. Without a will, that could end up being the public administrator, and the assets would be in a conservatorship, which I discussed earlier.

Once a conservatorship is set up and the assets are transferred to it, there is the question of how to invest the assets for the good of the children. Most parents would want the assets to be invested for a total maximum return within some conservative limits: nothing very risky – maybe some blue-chip stocks; maybe some bonds.

As I discussed earlier, with a conservatorship, that won't happen. The assets will be invested in CDs and money market funds; all government insured. Typically, those investments don't even keep up with inflation. The assets will actually be losing money against inflation.

And then there are expenses. The conservator cannot pay for food, housing, utilities, or anything without a court order, and the court will minimize expenses to conserve (prevent the wasting of) assets.

Finally, when each child reaches 18, they will get their separate share outright. That rarely seems to be a good idea. Even a relatively small amount to an 18-year-old is a fortune. As I discuss in other parts of this book, too much money too soon can ruin a child. Mercifully (?), I was saved from that burden.

Parents can avoid the consequences of a conservatorship by having a will. A will allows them to provide for a trust to take care of their children. Until the youngest child reaches a certain age, the assets can go into a common trust. Once the youngest child has reached the age where they should have completed college, then the common trust assets can be divided and distributed to separate trusts for the benefit of each child. Until they reach a certain age, you can appoint a trustee to handle the assets. Once they reach that age, they can be in charge. Problem solved.

Another instance when I have found a will alone to be the best plan is when an elderly person has very few children. I have worked with clients who are very elderly, who were actually in nursing homes. Everyone agreed that they would not be long with us. If they only have one or two children who are in good health, then maybe POD or TOD beneficiary designations is all they really need. The will is just a safety net.

So in certain circumstances a will may be the best estate planning tool. Along with the will, clients would also need a financial power of attorney and a medical directive, which I discussed earlier. I cannot imagine a time when no estate planning would be the solution. Instead, no planning is the first step to problems. That is what Suzy ran into in our story about Jack and Judy.

PLANS OF DISTRIBUTION

One of the questions clients struggle with all the time is how to distribute their estate. In the case of Jack and Judy, they decided to use joint ownership of their assets to achieve an equal distribution. We saw how that turned out.

Outright in equal shares sometimes makes sense, but what about when there are young children? What about when there are large sums of money? What if there is a special asset like a business or a vacation home? And what happens to your child's inheritance if they get a divorce?

Families are unique both as to their assets and the personalities and capabilities of the children. Although clients can go online to do their own estate planning, those programmatic documents might fit, but then again, they might not. I have seen lawyers set up similar on-the-cheap kinds of systems, but I can assure you that those system documents will do the very minimum for you. The old adage, "You get what you pay for," holds true. I have also seen lawyers charge large fees and shoe-horn their clients into a "one-size-fits-all" document off of their computerized system.

What I have seen is that clients do fit into some patterns that I have seen over time, but even then plans may need special drafting attention. What follows are several scenarios designed to illustrate some of the plans clients can consider. Not all of them will apply to anyone, but some will. Hopefully these stories will introduce some ideas to consider when planning an estate.

THE BASIC PLAN

Bob and Jamie have been married for many years. They have three kids, Joan, Margaret, and Jonathan. Joan and Margaret are 26 and 23, respectfully. They are both out of college and pretty good with money. Jonathan was a surprise blessing. He is 14. No one is really sure how he is going to turn out, but his sisters give him less than a 50% chance of ending up in the top half of his class. They could be wrong though.

Bob and Jamie were actually more proactive than most couples. When Joan and Margaret were very young, they had an attorney draft a will for them. Their main concern was who would get the kids. At the time, they named Jamie's sister, Amber, as the guardian. Objectively speaking, Amber would be a horrible guardian for Jonathan. She's not very patient, and she's used to girls.

They had not given a lot of thought to how to distribute their assets since at the time they wrote their wills, they were as poor as church mice in a poor parish. Their wills simply provided that whatever they had would be divided evenly between the kids. If the kids were under 18, the assets were to go to a trustee. But if they were over 18, then the assets were to be distributed outright.

Things were different now. They had been conservative about saving for retirement, and they had some life insurance payable to one another on their deaths. On their deaths, each of the kids would inherit over $250,000. That would have been fine for Joan and Margaret, but Jonathan was another story.

After reading a masterfully written book on estate planning, they decided to amend their estate plan. Since the attorney who wrote their will no longer practiced law, they decided to call an attorney who published columns in their local paper. The plan got fixed before it was too late.

The plan they adopted did call for an equal division of assets, but if the beneficiary (Jonathan) was under a certain age, his (or her) share would go into a trust with the older siblings as the trustees. Although that can create some life-long tension between the siblings and make for strained family gatherings (if any) in the future, they did not have any other good candidates in their families, and they did not want to have a trust company involved. Client rules.

BUT JASON GOT HIS

Mom and dad had been married for many years. They had three children whom they loved very much. The oldest, John, was married with a family. John and his wife didn't have much, but they'd been making it. They'd never asked for anything from mom and dad and had always been ready to help.

Their second child was Susan. Susan also was married with four children. Her husband had a good job and had been able to provide for their family, so Susan was a stay-at-home mom and raised the children, bringing them by for their grandma and grandpa to spend time with. Great joy for mom and dad.

Their youngest son was Jason. Jason had a tough life. His career never took off. His ex-wife got everything in the divorce. Mom and dad had financially bailed Jason out fairly often. They had spent a lot of money on Jason, and he was finally getting to a more stable point in his life.

When mom and dad went to see their attorney, they were sort of conflicted. They equally loved all of their kids, but it seemed to them (to different degrees) that Jason already had received his inheritance. Dad felt stronger about that than mom. And there was some resentment of Jason by John and Susan. When mom and dad did the math, they actually discovered that they had already given Jason much more than John and Susan would receive on their deaths.

In the end, mom and dad decided that Jason had already received his inheritance. They decided to leave their estate only to John and Susan. Mom was torn about this because she knew Jason would feel cheated, but she hoped that over time, he would understand. Still, it was a very difficult decision.

The law allows people to do basically whatever they want with their property on their deaths. Of course, without a pre-nuptial agreement, a person cannot disinherit his or her spouse. However, they can disinherit any one or more or even all of their children.

However, when a child is disinherited, you need to be careful. If you don't even mention them in your will or trust, the validity of the will or trust comes into question. As I discussed before, a person must be competent to write a will or a trust, and one requirement for competency is that the person must know the "natural objects of their be-neficence." If you don't mention all of your children, then that raises a question of competency.

But even if you mention them, that may not be the end of things. After the death of mom and dad, Jason may feel that John and Susan made mom and dad write him out of the will. Since he has nothing to lose, he could bring a will contest or trust contest lawsuit alleging undue influence or incompetency. There are plenty of attorneys who would take that case for one reason or another.

Under these circumstances, I would recommend that mom and dad leave Jason something. And the will or trust would include what is called an "in terrorem" clause. That clause says that if you sue and lose, you lose everything. If Jason sues to challenge the will or trust and loses, then he even loses the amount he was supposed to get. So it needs to be an amount or percentage that Jason could not ignore. So be afraid; be very afraid.

EVEN V. FAIR

It's probably a huge understatement to say that Cornelius Vanderbilt was an ambitious businessman. He grew up in a struggling family. He quit school at 11 to work for his father's ferry business in the New York Harbor. At 16, he started his own business, ferrying passengers between New York and Long Island. He built that small business into a major steamboat line, including ocean liners. After the Civil War, he switched to railroads and built that business into an empire. He was a fierce business competitor, running other businesses into the ground on occasion.

Vanderbilt was also reportedly an unpleasant man personally. He married a relative (a common practice in those days), and they had 13 kids. Because of business, Cornelius was often away from home. His wife and children lived in a large house on Staten Island. I read once that he even charged them rent. (Yes, you read that right.) She apparently had to take in boarders to pay rent and buy food and clothing for the children. He called his "favorite" son, William ("Billy"), a "blockhead" and a "blatherskite" (that's an old term for someone who talked a lot of nonsense). I'm not sure what he called his other children.

When he died, he was reportedly worth $100 million, which would be worth more than $227 billion in today's dollars. He didn't trust his kids with his financial empire, but he was stuck with Billy. He left Billy 95% of his estate. To one of his other sons he left $5 million, while two other sons received $2 million apiece. His nine daughters received amounts ranging from $250,000 to $500,000 (about $350 million to $700 million in today's dollars). He considered one son irresponsible, so he just got a trust fund worth about $200,000 (in today's dollars, over $250 million). His surviving wife (his second) also received a sizable inheritance, plus their house, plus a large block of railroad stock.

It's pretty clear to see that, even though everyone received sizeable amounts, this was not an even distribution. Needless to say, litigation followed. But Billy prevailed. Billy then proceeded to pay off all his siblings' legal fees and make substantial gifts to them. What a guy!

It turns out that Cornelius's choice of Billy was a good one. Under his stewardship, the family empire continued to grow. Within 6 years, he had doubled it to $200 million. In addition, Billy was a good philanthropist. He made sizable gifts to the YMCA, the Metropolitan Opera, and Columbia University. He also further endowed Vanderbilt University, which his father originally started. So for all involved, Billy was a good choice.

So what is the point of this story? Especially when there are family-held businesses, equal is not always the best policy. For instance, one child may be actively involved in the business, and the others know little or nothing about it. If everyone received an equal share (including an uninvolved child), then that would be a catastrophe for the family and the business.

Most parents who start a business want it to succeed down the generations. To do that, they need to give control and most of the profits to the person running the business.

He or she needs to have adequate incentives to put the sweat and tears into the business to make it work, just like the parents did. That means that the other family members need to get something of equivalent value, typically cash. You can do that with life insurance if the parents are young enough, or you can give the child who is operating the business an option to buy the business over time on favorable payment terms. If you use life insurance, you need to pay attention to estate taxes. The use of an irrevocable life insurance trust might make sense, but that discussion is beyond the scope of this book.

In any event, as I'll discuss later in this book, planning for the succession and success of the family business takes some time and careful considerations, taking into account both fairness and capabilities. Although Vanderbilt was dealing with much larger numbers, the same idea applies. Equality in everything may not lead to the best result.

TOO MUCH, TOO SOON?

Then there is the question of *when* to give children their inheritance. There used to be a fashionable restaurant in suburban St. Louis where some of my clients liked to meet for lunch. To get to the dining room, you had to go through the bar. I like to eat lunch around 11:30 to avoid the wait, so we'd be there before the rush.

As I would walk through the bar area late in the morning, I was always surprised at how many people (primarily older men) were sitting at the bar. It seemed as if they had been there quite some time, since they were well on their way to somewhere else.

One trust officer I know once referred to these gentlemen as "trust-babies." Their parents had made huge fortunes. They left their estates in trust to their children. All the kids had to do was collect dividends, royalties, and/or annuities. For a number of them, it seemed as if life had very few challenges, so they ended up sitting at a bar before 11:30 in the morning. I have clients who have resisted this temptation, but it takes a lot of will power.

Although we all want to provide for our kids, we don't want to ruin them, and large amounts of money, particularly at an early age, can do just that. Most of us can only wish we had to deal with vast sums of money, but wealth is a relative concept. Even smaller amounts can ruin teenagers and young adults.

In many studies of the formation and development of the brain in adolescents, neuroscientists have discovered that the frontal lobe of the brain – the part that asks, "Is this a good idea?" – isn't fully formed until we are in our mid-20s. For some people, I might argue, it is much later. Teenagers and young adults lack insight, that deeper understanding of the consequences of their actions.

It is also true that kids can develop bad habits that stick with them for life. We all probably do things repeatedly that we started doing when we were teenagers, and changing any of those habits is really tough. I believe that if we routinely act a certain way when we are young and our brains are more plastic, habits get ingrained.

I knew a kid in college who on his 21st birthday inherited not one but two insurance companies. Yes, they were small, but their stock dividends were more than a 21-year-old needed to have to live on. Even though he'd been a pretty good student before, he never finished school.

We work hard to accumulate wealth to take care of our families, yet that wealth may become a stumbling block (if not a barricade) to a productive life for our children. Careful planning can help avoid that. Certainly we should not just give young children a large sum of money outright. As I often tell my clients, we would've been prudent and responsible with a lot of money ourselves, but can we really trust our kids?

Until a child reaches an age of some maturity (and that age may be different for different children), I usually recommend that clients leave their money in a discretionary trust with an older relative or friend or a trust company as the trustee making investment and distribution decisions.

Who that trustee is depends on the size of your estate, and who your family members are.

And what is that age of maturity? I had one client who was offended by my suggestion that her 18-year-old son might not be able to handle his substantial inheritance. On the other hand, I had another client who didn't think that his children should be able to handle their inheritance until they were 62 ½. That age of maturity question is a tough one, and it varies from person to person. Careful planning is critical.

PROTECTING THE KIDS

Let's assume a couple goes to see their attorney. We'll call them Bill and Sandy. Let's further suppose they have four young kids, including a couple of teenagers. Two of the children are very good with money. One of them is okay, though the father had his concerns. The fourth never saw a nickel he couldn't spend. This is not an unusual family.

Bill's dad had died several years ago, and he left his mom pretty well-off. His mom had just recently died. Although she had spent a couple of years in a nursing home, Bill still inherited a nice sum. Between that and what Bill and Sandy had saved, their kids stood to inherit quite a bit of money as well. Bill and Sandy were worried.

When Bill was in high school and college, one of his best friends was Joe. Joe's mom had died when he was young, and Joe's dad had been pretty frugal and saved a lot of money. Because of his mother's early death, Joe had no brothers or sisters. His dad never remarried.

Soon after college, Joe's dad died tragically. He'd been young, so he had never thought to do any estate planning.

Everything went outright to Joe, and his life began a steep downhill spiral. He had no real direction or goals in life except to get more money out of his trust. I recently had a probate case where one of the sons had a drug habit. By law, we would have had to give him the money, but everyone knew that this would not end well. Bill and Sandy would not want that to happen to their kids.

The estate plan we would develop for Bill and Sandy would use a trust to avoid probate. Their assets would be completely under their control during their lives. On the death of the second of them to die, everything would be divided equally between their kids, but not distributed to them outright. Instead, Sandy's brother would be in control of the inheritance, and they could only get distributions for health, education, and maintenance in their standard of living. When the kids turn 35, they would get control. Bill and Sandy hoped that by then even the spender would have some money sense. In order to protect the kids from divorce claims and possible lawsuits, they decided to leave the kids money in trust for their lifetime while making the kids their own trustees at that time.

I have used this plan for many of my clients, and they are very relieved with it. It was the best plan Bill and Sandy could put in place to protect their kids.

TRUSTS

THE PROBLEM WITH PROBATE

When I meet with clients to talk about their estate planning, there are a lot of things to discuss. If there are minor children, then who will get the kids? If you don't name guardians, the court does that for you.

If they have life insurance, who will handle the money for the benefit of their family? If they fail to plan properly, then the court will set up a conservatorship. As I discussed earlier, someone you don't know may handle investments and distributions. Court approved investments are basically CDs and other government insured investments. Court-approved distributions are pretty narrow in scope, which may or may not be a good thing for your children. Since you won't know who is handling the money, you won't know if you can trust their judgment.

These issues can, of course, be addressed in either a will or a trust. Many people think that if they have a will, they'll avoid probate. That couldn't be further from the truth. With only a will, all assets in the decedent's name alone will have to be probated.

So the question is whether it's important to avoid probate. I usually give three reasons why clients want to avoid probate. The first is a loss of privacy. When you open a probate estate, you have to file the will. When the estate is opened, the court will send notices (including the will) to potential heirs and beneficiaries. I have literally had people come out of the backwoods of Minnesota claiming that Aunt Martha meant to leave them half of her estate.

We had trouble finding the guy in the first place, so there was no way he had been in touch with Aunt Martha. These notices can invite will contests.

Also, when you open a probate estate, the court will publish a notice in "a newspaper of general circulation." That's when the cards and letters start coming. People wanting to buy the house or invest the money.

Within 30 days after the estate is opened, the personal representative has to file an inventory of everything the decedent owned. Although there are some protections, probate is basically a public record. A persistent snoop can probably get to see the file. That is not helpful and can create problems for heirs. Wealthy (and that is a relative term) heirs appear to have a target on them.

Another reason why people want to avoid probate is the cost. Fees vary from state to state. Some states leave it up to the local judges to decide what is a "fair and reasonable" fee. If the attorney is a friend of the judge, his or her fees can be pretty high. In some states (such as Missouri), the fees are a percentage of the estate. As an example, if we assume a person owns a house, has a little IRA, and a little life insurance (all of which are probatable in this example), it's easy to have an estate worth $500,000 or more. Out of that pot of money, by statute Missouri allows the personal representative a fee of approximately $14,000. That same amount also goes to the attorney. Probate estates can be very profitable for lawyers.

The last reason to avoid probate is time. This was rather forcefully brought home recently when we were trying to open a probate estate. Even with all of the paperwork in proper form, it took almost 2 months to open the estate now that the process has been "automated." Once a person dies, his or her assets are frozen until an estate is opened. No bills can be paid, including the mortgage or utilities. Usually family kicks in and gets reimbursed, but that's kind of an imposition. And what if you have a business? That could kill it.

And once the estate is opened, in Missouri as in all states, it has to stay open for the claims period (as I discussed in the section on Probate) so any creditors can file claims. And if you didn't plan properly and authorize independent administration, then during the claims period, the only distributions that can be made are those that are approved by the court. After the expiration of the claims period, the personal representative has to file an accounting and a proposed order of distribution. Further delay! Most all of this can be avoided with a trust.

As you can see, there are plenty of reasons to plan your estate and consider a trust. But as I mentioned earlier, some surveys find that over 60% of the population has no estate plan at all. As some clients have said, "Why should I care? I'll be dead!"

But do you really want to leave your family a mess? Really?

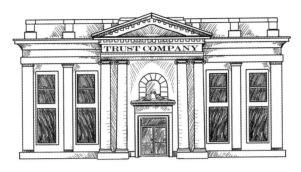

TRUST BASICS

As I discussed earlier, some people try to avoid probate by naming their children as beneficiaries of certain assets. Depending upon the asset, there are several questions to consider: 1) Do you want a 20-year-old to get a big life insurance distribution? 2) Will all of your children be able to work together to get your house ready for sale and then to sell it? 3) Do you want the IRA you worked so hard to build up to get taken by your child's creditors when he or she inherits it?

When I talk to clients about trusts, they usually are thinking about trusts managed by trust companies. The thought is that those are for rich people. Donald Trump probably has a trust. The Clintons also probably have one or more trusts. Those are for the Rockefellers and the Vanderbilts. Many times those impressions are pretty deeply embedded so they are hard to try to root out.

I know some attorneys who think that everyone should have a trust, and that probably is an overstatement. However, a trust is something that I think many people should consider for the reasons discussed in the previous chapter dealing with "The Problem with Probate." To do that, I think it would be helpful to understand a few trust basics.

Although we think about a trust as a thing, it's actually

just a contractual relationship between three parties. The first party is the person or persons who make the trust. They can alternatively be referred to as the grantor (my favorite and the way I will refer to them throughout this book), settlor, trustor, maker, etc. They all mean the same thing. This is the person or persons who own the assets that they want to entrust to someone else.

The second party to the trust contract is the trustee. This is the person to whom the grantor conveys the property. In law school, they tell us that the trustee does not really own the assets outright since they have to hold them for the benefit of another person (more on that in a second), so the trustee only has what is called "bare legal title." The trustee owes a fiduciary duty (as discussed earlier) to the beneficiaries of a trust. What that means is that the trustee is not free to do anything he or she may want with the trust assets. He or she can only administer them for the benefit of the beneficiaries. When a trustee uses assets for his or her own benefit, they will get sued. Any individual can be a trustee, but only a trust company (or a bank with trust powers) can be a corporate trustee.

The third party to the trust agreement is the beneficiary. Beneficiaries are the "persons" for whose benefit the trust assets are being held and administered. For our purposes, a "person" can be a child, an adult, a charity, or just about any individual or entity that exists. The grantor gets to define the benefits that are to be distributed. So the trust can: (i) payout only income; (ii) payout both income and principal; (iii) payout either income or principal only on the basis of some definition of need; (iv) be held for the life or lives of the beneficiary(ies); or (v) be paid out over a specific period of time. The law basically allows a lot of leeway. You just can't write a trust for an illegal purpose.

As I said, a trust is a three-party contractual arrangement involving a grantor, a trustee, and a beneficiary. However, by the magic of our legislatures, one individual can fill all of those roles. This is referred to as a "grantor trust." The grantor is the trustee and is the beneficiary. That way, one person or a married couple can create a trust for their own benefit and keep complete control of their assets.

But the question you might ask is, "Why bother?" Why go to all of this trouble to create a trust? The simple answer is that if a person creates and funds a trust, his, her, or their assets will be protected from a conservatorship during their lifetime and probate upon death. A trust bypasses all of that. A grantor saves time and money and avoids any publicity. The amount of money saved depends on the size of the estate and state law, but for estates over $500,000 (including your house, your retirement assets, your life insurance, and your investments), clients need to give serious consideration to trusts.

CHOOSING A SUCCESSOR TRUSTEE

Most clients, of course, want to remain in control of their assets for as long as they are able. That is why they are their own trustees.

But one of the stumbling blocks clients run into in planning their estates is who to put in charge at their death or incapacitation. This applies to almost any fiduciary, but here I want to look at it in the context of a successor trustee. Typically clients want to name family. Younger clients tend to name siblings. Parents tend to name their children.

In many cases, this can be a difficult decision. Who will be best at handling the fiduciary responsibilities of being a successor trustee (or a personal representative)? Who has the skills and knowledge? Who has the time? Who has the personality and the necessary people skills to do what you want?

Sometimes clients (parents in particular) are worried about hurting the feelings of a child or further alienating them from their other siblings. If you want things to go smoothly, I really think that these kinds of issues should almost never come to bear on this decision. However, if you insist on putting a child in charge who has already been alienated from their siblings, I think you're asking for disaster.

Sometimes clients don't want to leave anyone out of the loop, so they name some or all of their children as co-trustees. I almost universally discourage that. The administrative hassles are immense. Trying to get everyone to agree, even on simple matters, becomes a gargantuan task. Even if there are just two co-trustees, the possibility of deadlock is real.

Most of the time parents want to name their most successful child as the trustee. The problem with this is that Aaron, the neurosurgeon, lives out of town and really doesn't have the time, knowledge, or patience (not patients) to deal with these things—and it's not something he has ever done before. It's always good to learn a new skill set, right?

A lot of clients want to get whoever they are naming to agree in advance. That's a nice thought, although it is completely useless in my opinion. Although someone may or may not be interested in serving now, 10 or 20 years from now will almost certainly be an entirely different story. What I tell clients is that they can tell the people they have named that they've been named as the successor trustee of their trust after the fact, but insist that they are free to decline to serve. If it doesn't work when the time comes and the need arises, they should not feel obligated in any way if the burden would be too difficult. It's just that you trust them and believe that they can do a good job. I also tell them to blame the attorney for writing them in. It's always good to blame the attorney.

Then there's the question of what to do when there is no one who fits the bill. Or, what do you do if someone would kind of be a good fit, but not a real good fit? That's where a corporate trustee comes in.

In every case, even if we have 15 named individual trustees, I always want at least the final back-up trustee to be a corporate trustee, like a trust company. There is a chance that none of the 15 (and the chances are much greater with only two named successor trustees) will be willing or able to serve, or they may pre-decease you. If you only name individuals, and none of them will serve, then we will have to go to court to have a judge appoint a trustee. It could be the public administrator, and then the trust assets would be administered as a conservatorship, as we discussed earlier.

Corporate successor trustees (or even immediate corporate co-trustees) could be more appropriate under various circumstances. It may be that there are no family members who have the time or inclination to serve as trustee, and it would be too burdensome. It may be that the client doesn't trust any of his or her relatives. Potential family trustees may lack the knowledge or experience to serve as a trustee in a particular circumstance. And finally, tense family dynamics could make it impossible for a family member to serve as the sole trustee (or even maybe as a co-trustee).

There are several reasons to consider a corporate trustee. First, they are professionals at what they do. This shouldn't be minimized. Corporate trustees are held to a higher standard and are regulated both internally and externally. Another reason is that although individual trust officers may come and go, the corporate trustee itself doesn't die or become incompetent requiring a pretty involved transition, such as would be the case with individual trustees. Corporate trustees are also typically more objective since they are not entangled in family issues. They are a third party with an unbiased opinion. Finally, corporate trustees are experienced in all kinds of tax planning, record keeping, business, investment, and real estate dealings, which is not typically the case with individual trustees.

The issue that most clients raise with me is that corporate trustees will charge a fee. Depending on the institution and the size of the trust (the bigger the trust, the smaller the fee percentage), I have seen fees range from .60% (or even less for really big trusts) up to maybe 2%. When considering a corporate trustee, be sure to ask about minimum fees – some are prohibitive, though most are not. Also, be sure to ask about which services are included in the fee and find out about any extraordinary fees, such as termination fees. It is always a good idea to get the corporate trustee fee schedules – all of them. Finally, you probably want your family to be able to work with someone locally. If so, try to meet with them before you name them if you can.

With regard to trustee fees, it should be noted that individuals can be entitled to take trustee fees. After all, there is a lot of work involved. However, if professional investment advisors are being engaged (and they certainly should be), they will be charging a fee. If that is the case, then the individual trustee fee should be reduced by the amount of the professional investment advisor's fee so that the actual fee charge is comparable to a corporate trustee fee. However, individual trustees should be able to charge an appropriate fee.

As I mentioned above, naming a trustee can be a difficult and challenging decision. As with many estate planning questions, there is not a single answer that works for everyone because families are so different. Nonetheless, it is an important decision that must be made in planning an estate.

SPOUSES AND TRUSTS

Of the 50 states, nine have community property laws. These include Texas (my home state) and California, two of the most populous states in the nation. They have over 60 million residents out of about 320,000,000 in the US: about 20%. Probably because of that, most of the time when I see articles about married couples owning property together, the stories focus on community property. That is not the whole story.

A little over half of the states have some form of "tenancy by the entirety."

Most married couples own their property, whether real estate, bank accounts, investments (other than retirement accounts), or just about anything else, as "joint tenants." The full terminology for that is "joint tenants with right of survivorship." What this means is that when one owner dies, his or her interest in that property passes to the survivor automatically without the need for probate.

As I wrote earlier, generally speaking joint ownership can be a bad thing. With a bank account (where federal law applies), either joint owner can (and yes, they have) cash out the entire account and hightail it for the hills. With other assets (where state law applies), neither joint owner can do anything without the other joint owner(s) joining with them. In addition, if either joint owner gets sued, that account or piece of property can be taken to collect the debt.

The exception to the joint ownership problem is "tenancy by the entirety" ("TBE") property for married couples. TBE properly is property held jointly by spouses. In effect, it is not the property of either spouse separately. This law is a way to protect marriages and families. Marital property can only be taken to collect the joint debt of a married couple, but not the separate debts of married individuals. That's why a mortgage company always requires both spouses to sign off on a mortgage and loan.

Until recently in several states, estate planning with trusts posed certain problems for married couples. Without legislation, property held by a husband and wife in a joint trust lost that TBE protection. Although it didn't seem to make sense, if a husband and wife transferred their TBE assets into a joint trust, the transferred assets lost the TBE protection. Go figure. We planned around that with nonprobate transfer options, but it was not really a good solution.

Many legislatures have in fact fixed that problem. In Missouri the legislature created what are called "Qualified Spousal Trusts" ("QSTs"). A QST is a joint trust (and it doesn't matter when it was created) between a husband and wife. The trust must provide either that: (i) the trust assets are held and administered in one trust for the benefit of both spouses, the trust can be revoked by either or both spouses during life, and each spouse has the right to receive trust distributions; or (ii) the trust assets are held and administered in separate shares of a single joint trust for the separate spouses, with each share revocable by either spouse individually with respect to his or her share, and each spouse has the right to receive income from their separate share. Although this is kind of complicated, it's a great idea.

The one quirk in Missouri law for QSTs was that to obtain TBE protection in a QST, the property had to be transferred into the trust as TBE property. What that meant was that assets transferred into a QST as separate property did not receive TBE protection.

It's funny how many non-TBE assets people receive: direct deposit paycheck; pension payments; Social Security payments; and IRA distributions, just to name a few. When non-TBE assets were mixed with TBE assets, it looked like the QST protections were lost, although I never saw those cases. Still, it was a potential problem. We had strategies to work around this, but it was kind of clumsy.

We all kind of figured that the legislature would get around to resolving this odd situation, and over time, they did. Beginning in 2015, married couples could transfer non-TBE assets (whether real estate, bank accounts, or investments) into a QST and still receive TBE protection. This really simplifies the process for married couples with a joint trust. I like when we can simplify things for clients.

CHARLIE'S CHOICE

I clearly remember Charlie as he was leaving my office that day. He had just signed his trust, and I'd asked him if he wanted any help re-titling his assets into his name as trustee. With a twinkle in his eye, he smiled and said, "Don't worry. I'll take care of it," and he walked out my door.

Maybe three years later, Charlie's granddaughter called. Charlie had died as a result of a boating accident. Actually, it was a rafting accident. In March, while testing a raft on which he and some buddies were going to float down the Mississippi, a la Huckleberry Finn, he had fallen into Mark Twain Lake in northeast Missouri, caught pneumonia, and died. Charlie and his buddies were in their 80s. He certainly knew how to live life.

Charlie had named his granddaughter as his successor trustee and as the personal representative. I started to explain to her what was involved in administering a trust. I was talking about having to prepare a list of assets to start an inventory, and she interrupted me. She said Charlie hadn't done any of that stuff.

I was confused. She explained that Charlie had never funded this trust by re-titling his assets into his name as trustee. She told me he'd said that if he funded this trust, he felt that he would be telling God he was ready to die. Charlie wasn't ready to die, so he hadn't done anything. Now, everything needed to be probated.

Creating a trust is only the first part of a trust-based estate plan if one of your main goals is to avoid probate (which it almost certainly would be). Unless you also retitle your assets in your name (or in the case of a husband and wife, names) as trustee(s), the assets in an individual's name at his or her death will have to go through probate.

So what's involved in retitling assets into your trust?

There are two ways to transfer assets into a trust. Some states (including Missouri) allow you to just designate the trust, such as the "Betty Smith Trust." Maybe I'm being too formal or old-fashioned, but I don't like to do that.

You see, as I mentioned before, trusts do not technically "exist" like a corporation or an LLC. If you name a trust as the owner, you are naming a non-existent entity as the owner. The "person" who does exist is the trustee. So although you can name the trust, per se, as the owner, I think the better practice is to name the individual trustee as the asset owner: George Washington, Trustee of the trust for the benefit of Martha Washington, dated February 22, 1787.

We generally recommend that some assets be transferred directly into the trust. Investments and savings accounts fall into that category. Checking accounts may or may not be put directly into the trust. Some banks insist on putting "Trustee" on checks when an account is in a trust. That could raise questions at the grocery store. In those cases, you can add a POD beneficiary designation to your checking account.

The trustee should be named as the beneficiary for other assets. Use a beneficiary deed for your house and other property to make financing easier. Use a TOD beneficiary designation on your car to avoid problems with your lender and to simplify things with the license bureau. The beneficiary on life insurance should be the trustee (as trustee, of course) to avoid probate in case the grantors die close together in time. Name the trustee as the primary or contingent beneficiary of an IRA (yes, the IRS allows this as discussed earlier) to avoid accelerating the tax on your IRA assets. You just need to make sure the trust has the magic language the IRA promulgated in 1999.

You can also avoid probate by naming individuals as either joint owners or as direct beneficiaries, but this defeats the purposes of the trust and creates other problems, as I have discussed in other chapters.

The moral of the story is that to avoid problems, fund your trust. Otherwise, you (and your beneficiaries) may end up paying your attorney more than you intended.

CHARITABLE
PLANNING

For much of my career as an estate planning attorney, I've worked with primarily religious charities using estate planning ideas to raise money for their mission and ministry. There are some very goodhearted people out there who quietly make very generous gifts to churches, colleges, and foundations. For many of these charities, these are a sustaining resource.

In this book, I don't want to get into all of the details of gift annuities, unitrusts, donor advised funds, or endowments. They can get fairly technical and will probably put most readers to sleep. However, I do want to share some stories about a few of the people I've been blessed to meet while doing this work.

ESTHER'S GIFT

Esther was in a bad marriage. Her husband drank a lot, and when he was drunk... well, let's just say it was a bad marriage.

He couldn't hold a job, so Esther did what she could to support them. One day she happened to see a University of Tennessee football game. She didn't know the first thing about football, but she thought the cheerleader uniforms were really cute. She had an idea.

She put her dilapidated sewing machine on the kitchen table, and she started to sew. She sewed several different sizes of little girl versions of the cheerleader uniforms. Then she went to the University of Tennessee bookstore. She showed the little uniforms to the manager, who scoffed at them. But Esther was so persuasive, the manager agreed to take them on consignment. No investment on her part; but if they sold, she agreed to pay Esther.

That was a good weekend for the University of Tennessee. They won their game. Whenever that happens, the bookstore is busy. And that weekend, they were particularly busy.

Early Monday morning Esther's phone rang. It was the bookstore manager. It turns out that all of Esther's little uniforms had sold. In fact, there were backorders. The manager placed a big order.

But Esther had a problem. She only had one old sewing machine, 24 hours in a day, and a big order. So she talked to a few friends there in Alamo, Tennessee, and they came to help, all bringing their own dilapidated sewing machines. Sewing in Esther's kitchen, they filled that order, and more orders came in from the bookstore.

It's hard to keep a good thing quiet, and college football is really competitive. Several other schools heard about what Esther was doing and tracked her down. She even got orders from the University of Alabama. Although she intensely disliked Alabama, she sucked it up and filled the orders. Maybe she charged a premium.

She had more orders than she and her friends could fill out of her kitchen and dining room. The local bank gave her a loan, and she built an extension off her kitchen. Pretty soon, 25 of the local ladies were sewing little cheerleader outfits with new sewing machines, even uniforms for hated rivals.

A man from a neighboring state heard about Esther's business, and he came to visit her. He had this idea about a chain of stores. Esther didn't necessarily understand everything he said, but she liked Sam. She also had more money than she had ever imagined. She bought some Walmart stock. Needless to say, she did well with that investment. Who says investing is hard?

I never heard what happened to Esther's husband, but he evidently quietly moved out of the picture.

Esther was getting older. She didn't have any children. She wasn't interested in leaving her estate to her nieces and nephews. A lot of money (or even a little money in Alamo, Tennessee) can really ruin a kid.

There are a lot of things that motivate people to give to charities. Sometimes it's just a sense of altruism... it's the right thing to do. Other times it's a desire to leave a legacy and have a building named after them.

In Esther's case, she was a religious woman. She recognized that God had had a hand in creating her wealth. So she contacted her church about creating an endowment.

When I met her, she was pretty much out of the business. She came to meet me in St. Louis so she could go to a Cardinals game. She'd only heard the games on the radio. Having no connections, I was only able to get tickets for seats way at the top of the stadium, in left field. Still, she was ecstatic.

Her endowment has helped several poor congregations in her denomination and has supported several outreach ministries. Without her gift, none of that would have happened. It's funny what a little idea can grow into and how much good you can do with it. As far as she was concerned, Esther had received a gift from God, and she only wanted to give it back. What a concept!

HENRY'S LEGACY

Henry was born and raised on a farm in Florissant, Missouri. For those of you who aren't familiar with Florissant, Missouri, it is smack-dab between the Missouri River and the Mississippi River, the two biggest rivers in America. Although he lived very close to both of these major waterways, he never learned to swim. When World War II broke out, he was drafted early on, into the Navy, of course. Sink or swim! And he swam.

Henry was assigned to the admiral's battleship in the Pacific. He had a good voice, so he became the radio operator. The radio room was near the bottom of the ship. Even during the roughest storms, he just rocked gently back and forth.

The captain heard his voice and decided he needed to be on the bridge piping orders to the crew. When an officer told him to report to the bridge, Henry explained that he liked his job. Evidently that isn't relevant in the Navy.

The first thing Henry noticed on the bridge was that his chair had a seat-belt. When he asked what that was for, the officer said with an evil grin, "Oh, you'll find out." Henry found out alright. In bad storms that gentle rocking in the radio room became the worst roller coaster ride you could imagine on the bridge. That seat-belt came in very handy.

On a Navy ship, the bridge gives you a view of most of what happens on the deck. Henry watched incredible scenes of bravery from the sailors during battles. He saw men coming onto the ship from transports fall from their rope ladders and get eaten by sharks. And he saw the cursing kamikaze pilots after their wing controls had been shot out as they flew past the ship, only to crash into the ocean. He was usually the last person any of them ever saw. Henry had incredible stories to tell.

But Henry didn't have any children to tell the stories to. When he got back to the States after the war, he married, but he and his wife couldn't have children. So he ended up telling the stories to me.

But more than that, Henry left a legacy in another way. As they were nearing the end of their lives, he and his wife decided to give their estate to a university to set up an endowed scholarship. I had the privilege to help them plan their estate and worked with the successor trustee to fund the scholarship on the death of the second of them to die.

As my wife says, everyone has a story. The problem is that upon our deaths, our stories can go silent. One way to continue the story is through an endowment to a charity. It's just something to think about.

GIVING YOUR CAKE AND EATING IT TOO

I was approached by a client several years ago about a piece of real estate he owned out in the country. A neighbor of his had approached him about selling it, but he had a problem. The land had been gifted down to him through several generations of his family. As a result of this, if he sold the land, he would have had a big capital gains tax. The property wasn't generating any income, so he liked the idea of selling it, but he didn't want to lose a fourth of it in taxes.

I asked him if he had any charities he favored. He said that he did, and he had remembered one of them in his trust. That was perfect.

I talked to him about a lifetime charitable remainder trust. So long as he didn't already have a binding contract to sell the land, he could transfer the property to a trust and get a tax deduction (he could even be his own trustee), sell the property out of the trust without incurring any immediate capital gains taxes, invest 100% of the sales proceeds, and earn an annual "unitrust amount" (a percentage of the trust principal's fair market value) for the rest of his life and the life of his wife. On death, the remainder would pass to his charity.

He thought about it for a little while and asked a bunch of questions. In a way, it sounded too good to be true. In the end though, he created the trust, sold the property, and started receiving income he hadn't been expecting. In this day and age, a little extra income can go a long way.

He also became a hero at his church. They were going to receive a substantial gift at some point in the future, and they were grateful.

The client got to give away his cake and eat it too. This was a win, win, lose result. The client won; the church won; and the IRS lost, which is always a good thing.

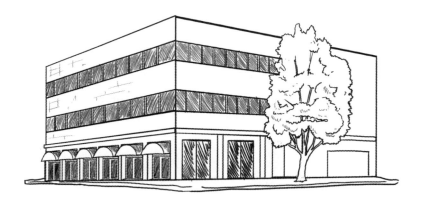

BUSINESS
PLANNING

AT THE BEGINNING

For business owners, many times their largest asset is their business. If the owner is going to plan his or her estate, they have to take the business into account. A discussion of estate planning for business owners can be divided into two parts. The first part has to do with planning at the time of the formation of the business. This is what we will look at in this chapter. The second part has to do with family planning and planning for death with wills and trusts. I'll look at that in the next chapter.

BUY/SELL AGREEMENTS

When two or more people go into business together, they are focusing on sales, production, costs, profits, and those kinds of things. Most of their focus is on the short term, immediate issues. That is understandable, but potentially risky.

If you're old enough, we can trade stories about people we know who died early and many times suddenly. If you're not old enough to know people who suddenly died, listen to your elders!

Business owners who fail to plan for a potential death run the risk of ending up in business with the co-owner's spouse or children. Typically, the spouses are not involved in the business, but of course, they have a lot of advice for you after the fact. I don't think I've ever seen a time when things have gone well after the death of a business partner when there was no real planning. When an uninvolved spouse becomes active in the business due to a sudden death, it usually means the end of the company. Planning for this eventuality is really important.

In this discussion, I am generically talking about buy-sell agreements, whether we are dealing with a C-corporation, an S-corporation, an LLC, or a partnership. I will simply refer to them as businesses. These ideas apply to them all.

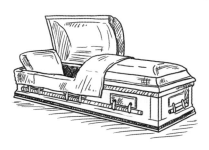

DEATH

Although the title of this section may sound kind of ominous, this really is an important part of planning for a business. If an owner were to die suddenly, the surviving owner or owners need to have a way to buy back their deceased co-owner's interest in the business and often-times to provide funding to transition to a new manager of some sort.

Typically in buy-sell agreements, the estate of a deceased owner will be required to sell his or her interest back to the business or the other owners (a discussion of which one is right for a particular business is beyond the scope of this chapter). The first question is value: how much is the business interest worth? Should the owners try to agree or should they use an outside appraiser or accountant? Once that is determined, then the owners need to plan on how to pay the purchase price. Many times that is funded by life insurance (whether owned by the business or by the owners is a whole other discussion), which may be the best way to handle this. If there are no life insurance proceeds or insufficient proceeds, the deficit can be paid over a designated period of time. It is important that all of this is worked out in advance. Otherwise, you can have an ownership meltdown at a time when you least need that to occur.

DISABILITY

Disability is a little more complicated. Valuation is still a problem, but funding the buyout is a problem. That can be funded with a disability policy payable to the company, or it can be paid out of future company profits. Also, if there is a life insurance policy with cash value, you can use the cash value to purchase the business interest. In any event, this will probably need to be paid out over time.

VOLUNTARY TRANSFERS

Finding a business partner in the first place is really tough. You really don't want to be in business with just anyone. Will they be honest? Will they work hard enough? Do they know what they are doing? Another aspect of a buy-sell agreement is what is called a right-of-first-refusal.

Since business owners don't want to be in business with just anyone, they will usually prohibit each other from selling the business interests – whether shares of stock, units (or whatever) in an LLC, or a partnership interest – to third parties. However, the courts will not enforce just an outright prohibition. That kind of restraint on trade is not welcome in American business. The typical way to prevent such a transfer is to impose a "right-of-first-refusal."

What happens with a right-of-first-refusal is that when one co-owner receives an offer to buy his or her business interest, that co-owner must first present that offer to the other owners and give them the right to buy the selling owner's interest on substantially the same terms. The remaining owners can pay the purchase price over time, but they still have to buy the co-owner's interests. The remaining owners can buy the selling owner's interest either directly or through the business or both, depending on how you set up the buy-sell agreement. An important aspect to remember though is that no matter what, all of the selling owner's interests that are being offered should be purchased by the remaining owners or the company. You can't only buy a part of the interests being offered. Another possibility is that if neither the company nor the owners accept the offer, then the remaining owners could require the sale of the entire business.

There is a lot involved in setting up a business when there are multiple owners, and the buy-sell agreement is an important part of it. In the next chapter, I will look at estate planning more specifically.

PLANNING FOR THE END

In the last chapter I focused on the planning that people need to do at the beginning of their business with a buy-sell agreement. Now I want to turn to the kind of planning that is more proper to estate planning at the end of one's life.

THE BiG TRANSiTiON

It has been estimated that over the next 30 years, an estimated $30 trillion (yes, that's "trillion" with a "T") will be passed from the baby-boom generation to the younger generations. For many people, that will consist of houses (some boats and fewer airplanes), life insurance proceeds, investments, retirement assets, personal property items, and yes, their businesses.

About half of the US economy is made up of small businesses, however you define that. On just a numeric basis, the SBA estimates that 99.7% of all employees are employed by small businesses. That is a large number of small businesses. Now admittedly, a large portion of those businesses may be businesses without employees, but that includes partnerships and LLCs. So there are still a lot of closely held businesses out there that could be passed down to the younger generation.

Beginning back in the 1990s, we began hearing a lot about how all of these family business owners were going to start planning to pass their businesses down to their children. Since those plans often involve life insurance, all of the life insurance agents were getting excited. The problem is, I'm not seeing it.

I talk to a lot of small business owners. The first question in planning an estate with the business interest is whether any kids are active in the business. If there are no kids, are there any key employees? If the client has neither, then they probably would just want to sell. If they enjoy running the business, then they may want to stay at the helm, die at the desk, and let others deal with the aftermath.

You might have a client who wants to stay involved, but also wants to travel or have more personal time. In that case, he or she may want to sell the business, but have a long term consulting contract that includes an office with a desk. These can be difficult arrangements, though. It's hard for people to give up the reins. There can be a lot of tension between the new owner and the "consultant." This kind of arrangement requires just the right people.

And then you might have a client who just wants out. That's when you clearly sell. Selling a business is beyond the scope of this discussion, but it's an option to consider. It's the "now versus later" option.

But let's say that there is a family member or a trusted employee in the mix. Then there is another analysis you need to consider.

FAMILY MEMBERS

I recently had a client business owner come in to see me regarding his estate planning. The 800-pound gorilla in his estate planning closet was his business. That's the way it is with most small business owners.

In reviewing their assets, they have a house. They have some investments. But their principal asset is their business. Business owners often don't even have a 401(k), an IRA, or any other kind of retirement asset. Their business is their retirement plan.

This client who came in had a son in the business. Even though his son was in the business, his son had some unrealistic ideas about what it took to run the business. So we had to ask some very basic questions:

- What if the business fails?
- Can your son get a loan on his own?
- Is your son willing to guarantee 100% of an SBA loan and is the client willing to take back a subordinated part of the purchase price in the process?

In that particular situation, the client had to get value out of the business. He was dependent on it for his retirement. He was not willing to just sell it to his son because he wasn't sure that his son would make it.

In addition, he did not think his son would be able to get a loan. His son had little collateral because he spent everything. Even if the son qualified for an SBA loan, he didn't think his son and his son's wife wanted to guarantee the loan and risk everything. In addition, an SBA loan would only cover 90% of the appraised value. The parents really needed 100% of the appraised value to make their retirement work. They could take back a subordinated note for the difference, but that was not really good enough. So the SBA loan option would not work.

In the end, the couple just decided to put the business up for sale. Their son was not happy, so they gave him some time to work out financing, but he couldn't get it ... at least not on his terms. The business ended up getting sold, and the son had to get another job.

SELLING TO A CHILD

These are the kinds of real life issues business owners face in planning their estates. It's always a risk to sell the business to a family member. One business owner sold his business to a child and took back a note and security agreement. He and his wife then moved to Hawaii... for a while, at least. The child was either overwhelmed by running the business or she just didn't put in the time (there are two versions to this story), but in any event, she started having trouble making the payments to her parents. Mom and dad moved to Florida to be closer and give some guidance. That didn't work either.

In the end, mom and dad moved back to St. Louis, declared a default, and took the business back. Dad had to rebuild the business and sell it to a third party for a reasonable price. Needless to say, relations with their daughter were a little chilly after that.

THE OTHER KIDS

And then there is the problem of the other children. As I mentioned earlier, many times the family business is the main asset in the estate. Typically small business owners don't put money away into retirement plans, so the business is the retirement plan. That can actually work since the proceeds from the sale of the business will be taxable at capital gains rates and not ordinary income rates, but that assumes that mom and dad can get their money out of the business, as I discussed above.

So if we assume that little Johnny is going to get the business, then the $1,000,000 question is "What about the other kids?" If Johnny pays cash for the business (either out of his own pocket or from a loan), then the other kids get cash, and that may be what they want. They never trusted little Johnny that much anyway.

But what if the company is a cash cow and is on autopilot so that even Johnny can't screw it up? Maybe the other kids want a piece of the action? Does Johnny want them meddling in "his" business?

In the alternative, what if Johnny can't pay what the business is worth or mom and dad decide to just self-finance the sale? Then the other kids don't get cash; they get a piece of a promissory note. Hopefully it is secured by the business. But do the other children really trust their inheritance with Johnny?

As with many estate plans, there is not a one-size-fits-all solution. A lot depends on the many intangibles and variables in the family and the business itself. Do the children get along? Do they like and/or trust each other in the business setting? Is one of the kids experienced at running the business? Is the business doing well with a bright future or is it struggling? If it is struggling, is this a temporary problem or a long-term one? Once you answer some of these questions, you can begin to put together a real plan.

When I was young, my mother often told me, "Remember Fred: blood is thicker than money." As a 10 year old, I had no idea what she was talking about. Now I wonder what happened in her family that had made such an impression on her. I'll never know now.

But needless to say, she was right. As with most estate plans, I don't think you know if it is successful until mom and dad have been dead for several years. Then you can ask, "Are the kids still celebrating holidays together?" If not, and it is because of hurt feelings from the estate plan, then it wasn't a good plan. If so, then the plan worked well...or at least as well as could be expected.

DIVORCE AND
SECOND MARRIAGES

YOURS, MINE, AND OURS

When I was young, the typical family was a mother and father and a couple of kids. Things weren't perfect, but they were pretty stable. Now I think that is more the exception than the rule.

Today, I run into Ward and June Cleaver less and less. Deaths and divorce make life difficult, and remarriages can make life complicated. It would be nice if everyone just got along, but apparently they don't. The emotional and financial aspects of blended families can be very complicated. Divorced individuals and remarried couples need to give some careful thought to their situations for estate planning purposes.

Divorcees are often happy to hear that for inheritance purposes, their ex-spouse will be treated as having predeceased them. No further comment on that.

However, that is not the end of it. If the couple during their marriage had kids, on the death of the first ex-spouse to die, minor children will have to go to the surviving ex-spouse unless he or she has renounced his or her parental rights. But the remaining question is who gets the kids on the death of the second ex-spouse to die. As I've mentioned before, I don't think that you would want to leave that decision to chance or to a judge. If the ex-spouses can't agree on who should be the guardian on the death of the second of them to die, then the survivor of them gets to decide.

If you did estate planning during your marriage, you will want to check to see who will manage things on your death. In most relationships, one spouse is usually the one who calls the shots. He or she may have persuaded the other spouse who should be named as the personal representative of your estate or the trustee of the trust for your kids. However, after the divorce, you probably don't want your ex-brother-in-law anywhere near your estate or your kids.

And then there is remarriage.

Doing nothing is not a good option. Doing nothing might mean leaving premarital assets in separate names. What happens on the death of the first spouse depends on how his or her assets were held, and whether there were beneficiary designations. In Missouri at least, if there are minor children and the assets were in the name of the deceased spouse alone, the surviving spouse may only get the first $20,000 and half the balance. If there are no minor children and no will, then the surviving spouse gets everything, and the children get nothing. But it will certainly require probate. If the deceased spouse designated beneficiaries on assets, then the surviving spouse may have rights in those assets, but probably not without a fight.

On the other hand, doing nothing might mean putting all of their property in joint names. In that case, as I discussed earlier, the surviving spouse and his or her children get everything. As I mentioned in the section on joint property, that is a tough conversation to have with the children of the deceased spouse when they find out that they are getting nothing.

Upon divorce or remarriage, clients need to pay attention to their estate plans. Who gets the kids? Who handles wrapping things up? Who handles the money after you're gone or even when you become disabled? And what happens to your estate if you remarry?

Careful planning with an attorney is important in order to avoid emotional and financial train wrecks. Don't put it off.

PRENUPTIAL AGREEMENTS

I get calls from prior clients who are thinking about remarriage. They tell me that although they love their intended and want to take care of him or her, they also are concerned about how to protect their kids' inheritance. They don't necessarily want their hard-earned money to go to their intended's kids. That might change over time, but that is generally not the case in the beginning.

If a person has children by a prior marriage and is getting remarried, the best way to protect those kids is with a prenuptial agreement. Many (if not all) state laws allow for post-nuptial agreements as well, but you'll want to check that out in your local state. For purposes of this discussion, I'm going to refer to either type of these agreements as "prenuptial agreements." In either case, the requirements are basically the same: after full disclosure by both parties of all of his or her financial resources, each spouse must knowingly and affirmatively waive any and all legal rights they may have in the other spouse's property. However, it should be noted that even with that, a judge may not enforce the agreement.

The general idea is that the court will respect a valid agreement between two parties to give up specified legal rights. In order for these to be valid contracts, there has to be somewhat equal bargaining positions – one party can't force the other party to do something. Also, each party must give adequate consideration – such as money, property, mutual promises, or some other benefit – to the other party. The law does not favor, and the courts will not enforce, particularly one-sided contracts. For instance, if Prince Charming (or not-so-charming) had required Cinderella to sign a prenuptial agreement where she agreed to get nothing if they ended up not living so happily ever after, a court would probably not enforce that. Sometimes people talk about spouses having an unequal bargaining position, but it strikes me more as a lack of consideration issue.

It cannot be emphasized enough that one of the best ways to make a prenuptial agreement meaningless is for one or both of the clients to fail to disclose any and all assets owned. The disclosure not only needs to be complete, but it also needs to be meaningful for the other party. If all you do is you list some obscure asset, and even when questioned about it fail to adequately disclose the nature of the asset and the value, a court is not going to respect that. So a complete and meaningful disclosure of any and all assets an intended spouse owns needs to be listed on an exhibit to the prenuptial agreement.

In addition to giving up rights, prenuptial agreements can also lock certain rights in place. For instance, many times, even with a prenuptial agreement, the spouses want to provide for the surviving spouse's health and maintenance if they are still married at the time that one of the spouses dies. You don't necessarily want to give the surviving spouse complete control of the assets, but setting some or all of the one spouse's assets under the control of an independent or related third-party trustee makes sense.

As I mentioned at the beginning of this section, a prenuptial agreement is the best way to protect the interest of children from a previous marriage. In the agreement, each spouse must waive any claims of his or her survivors in the other spouse's separate property. That way, each spouse will be free to leave their separate property to his or her children or other beneficiaries without the interference of the other spouse's descendants.

The other issue that needs to be addressed in a prenuptial agreement is who gets what in a divorce. That discussion is beyond the scope of a book on estate planning, so I'll leave that to someone else at some other time. You just need to make sure that the issue is covered.

So although prenuptial agreements can be a challenge to address during the courtship phase of a relationship, sometimes it is critically important that something be done. Hopefully a little education will help.

Ideally there would always be a prenuptial agreement, especially when there are kids by prior marriages. But let's be real. Who wants to go through the chilling waters of a pre-nup during a budding romance? It just doesn't happen that often, no matter what your advisors might tell you.

I once had a 79-year-old client whose husband died. She had a sizeable estate. Knowing her as I did, I told her that if she met someone, she needed to get a prenuptial agreement before tying the knot. She called me about 6 months later to tell me that she had married a guy she had met at a trailer park. Some people just don't listen.

PREMARITAL TRUSTS

When clients just can't deal with a prenuptial agreement for one reason or another, as a backup plan, I have sometimes suggested that they have us prepare a premarital trust. It doesn't solve all the problems, but it does address some.

The idea with a premarital trust is that the one spouse creates a grantor trust before the marriage. The grantor spouse should make the trust discretionary to provide for his or her health, education, and maintenance. It would be best to have either a separate trustee, or at least an independent co-trustee, but clients don't like to give up control.

The trust can even include provisions for the intended spouse on the grantor's death, so long as they were married and not legally separated at the time of the grantor spouse's death. In addition, those benefits could terminate on remarriage. On the death of the second spouse to die, all of the grantor spouse's remaining assets could go to his or her children, or other descendants of the deceased grantor spouse.

I am not a family law attorney who handles divorces, but I have partners who do handle them. They've told me that in the event of a divorce, provided that the grantor spouse has kept the pre-marriage assets separate from the joint marriage assets, the assets in the trust are not marital assets includable in the divorce proceedings. So long as you don't put post-marriage assets in the pre-marriage trust, the new spouse will only have such rights in those assets that you may give him or her. If you put post-marriage assets in that trust, then things can get complicated. So premarital trusts can protect premarital assets from divorce claims.

Death, however, is another matter. Although I have not seen any cases on this, it seems that unless the survivor spouse has effectively waived their rights in the grantor spouse's estate and/or trust, the surviving spouse would have the right to a portion of the deceased spouse's assets by electing against the will. For that reason, a premarital trust is not the best solution.

SCOUNDRELS, THIEVES, AND OTHER MISCREANTS

FINANCIAL EXPLOITATION OF THE ELDERLY AND DISABLED

Financial abuse of the elderly and disabled is a growing problem. With the increasing number of small, alienated families in our society, there are any number of con artists trying to relieve the elderly and disabled of their property. These classes of people are particularly susceptible to exploitation because they are almost desperate for help.

In the past, these cases of financial abuse were difficult to prosecute. The victims often failed to make a complaint and when someone else started proceedings, the victims would even testify on behalf of the perpetrator. It was kind of the "Stockholm Syndrome," when the hostage or kidnap victim develops feelings of trust or even affection towards their captors.

Recognizing this problem, many states (including Missouri, beginning in 2017) have passed laws that make this kind of financial exploitation of the elderly or disabled a crime. These laws vary from state to state, and I will not undertake a complete survey of them. Instead, I am going to talk about the law here in Missouri. If you live elsewhere, you'll need to check your local laws.

In Missouri, to prove this crime, the police only have to show that the perpetrator through deceitful means obtained control over the victim's property with the intent of permanently depriving the victim of the property for the benefit of the offender or the detriment of the victim. Depending on the amount in controversy, the crime can be classified as a misdemeanor up to a Class A felony.

The law specifically exempts people who try to make a good-faith effort to help an elderly or disabled person, but were unable. In addition, the law specifically exempts legitimate tax planning initiatives, so long as they don't harm the person's standard of living.

However, the law makes it a crime for an individual to fail to pay over funds belonging to a Medicaid eligible elderly or disabled person to the residential facility where he or she is then living. This may make some forms of Medicaid planning criminal. The law allows a court to order restitution of all funds unlawfully withheld from such a facility.

It is important to note that this law only makes criminal certain lifetime financial exploitations. Except in the case of Medicaid fraud, the law does not specifically mention restitution. It only criminalizes lifetime financial exploitation of the elderly and disabled. For instance, if a person through deceit convinces an elderly or disabled person to appoint them as their attorney-in-fact and then transfers all of their bank accounts into their own separate, individual accounts, then this law would probably come into play to criminalize the actions. It does not specifically call for restitution. However, to recover "stolen" funds or to terminate an invalid will or trust, further legal proceedings would be necessary.

WILL AND TRUST CONTESTS

As I mentioned in the preceding chapter, the laws passed to protect the vulnerable from financial exploitation have a fairly limited application. They make certain actions criminal, but they really don't fix the problem. Further legal action is necessary to do that.

We recently became involved in a case in which a "friend" had convinced a very ill elderly gentleman to appoint her as his agent under a durable power of attorney. The next day she emptied his bank accounts.

The man's son called to find out what he could do to recover the assets. The process to do that is to file what is called a "discovery of assets" petition. This petition can be filed either during a person's life or after their death by their estate. The theory is that the perpetrator took advantage of the victim, stole the assets, and needs to return them.

If it turns out that the assets weren't taken during the decedent's lifetime, but that the decedent signed a will or a trust that did not truly reflect his or her wishes, then a will or trust contest is the proper procedure. In either proceeding, the plaintiff has to show that the will or the trust is invalid for some reason. The more common reasons for this are lack of competency (which we discussed earlier) or undue influence. Sometimes these are so intertwined that it is almost impossible to distinguish one from the other.

In the case of undue influence, the plaintiff needs to show that the decedent was dependent on the alleged perpetrator. In the alternative, the plaintiff can show that the decedent placed his or her trust in the alleged perpetrator. In either case, the plaintiff will need to show that the perpetrator took advantage of his or her position and benefited from it.

In these cases, one of the problems both sides will have is that the main witness is either dead or incompetent. That usually makes the gathering of evidence circumstantial. As you can imagine, these cases are very hard to prove one way or the other. For that reason, before commencing this kind of a lawsuit, the family needs to be pretty certain about the facts. The process of discovering the facts will probably be difficult. Since the perpetrator will certainly assert capacity and deny undue influence, these cases often come down to a "he said/she said" kind of argument.

Although these cases are not easy to win, they are not impossible. They just take time. Although clients typically want a quick result, they need to be patient as the case is built from the facts that are discovered. Litigation can be painful.

SPECIAL
QUESTIONS

ESTATE TAXES

For the majority of my legal career, I have spent a substantial amount of time talking to clients about estate taxes. Estate taxes hit a number of people just because of a life insurance policy they may have had. Back when the exemption amount was $600,000, a million-dollar life insurance policy could result in a $160,000 tax bill. No one liked that.

However, although I still have clients asking me about the estate tax, back in 2010, Congress raised the "exemption amount" (the amount that can pass tax-free to your heirs) to $5,250,000. This amount is also indexed for inflation. It is currently around five and half million dollars. For the vast majority of Americans (99.9% according to some pundits), the federal estate tax is irrelevant.

It is possible that Congress could lower the exemption amount. However, that seems unlikely to me. The people who pay for election campaigns are the wealthy people who would be taxed. With the exception of some prominent billionaires, none of those people want to elect someone who will end up costing their families millions. Even though I don't think that the federal estate tax will impact many Americans, in the interest of full disclosure, I will give a brief outline of it.

In calculating a person's taxable estate, the IRS pulls in just about everything. Your house, any real estate you might own, bank accounts, cars, equipment, and investments (even your IRAs and 401(k)s) are all brought in. Any annuities or life insurance policies in which you had an "incident of ownership" (and that phrase has been ripe for litigation) are brought in. If you had a "power of appointment" (the right to say where someone else's property should go on their death), that property is included. Some trust interests (such as grantor trusts) are brought in as well. In effect, almost anything you had some kind of an interest in (no matter how insignificant) can be added into your taxable estate.

The next question is valuation. Typically assets are added in at fair market value. For real estate, that requires an appraisal. Stocks, bonds, and other securities actively traded on an exchange can be valued at their traded values. Closely held business interests have to be appraised, and the IRS scrutinizes those very closely. Sometimes we try to fragment ownership interests to get "lack of control" and "lack of marketability" discounts, but that discussion is beyond the scope of this book.

There is a relatively new thing you might've heard about: portability. What that means is that on the death of the first spouse to die, the surviving spouse (by filing a form) can move the deceased spouses unused exemption amount over to his or her estate and effectively double their exemption without doing any prior planning. My issue with portability is that the decedent's exemption amount (which would otherwise increase with inflation) is locked in to the exemption amount as of his or her date of death. It does not increase with inflation.

There are very few deductions allowed in calculating the taxable estate. You can deduct debts, funeral expenses, and the costs of administering the estate. You can deduct amounts passing outright to a surviving spouse or in certain restricted trusts ("QTIP Trusts") for the benefit of the surviving spouse. In addition, charitable contributions are deductible.

Once you have corralled the assets, valued them, taken your deductions, and then reduced the taxable estate by the exemption amount, the net estate is taxed at 40%. That is still a big number for those with taxable estates, but as I said it is irrelevant for the vast majority of Americans.

Although I wonder whether politicians will try to change the estate tax, a word of caution might be appropriate. It's easier to tax dead people than the living. Both of the political parties are talking about changing the estate tax regimen in some way. In addition, both are talking about doing away with the date of death step-up in basis. That being said, caution is the watchword. Be alert and pay attention to any laws proposed to change the estate tax, and plan accordingly.

OLD TRUSTS, NEW PROBLEMS

Before about the year 2000, when the estate tax exemption amount began increasing by leaps and bounds, we wrote a lot of estate plans with tax planning included. As in many non-community property states, we would create separate trusts for the husband and wife. On the death of the first of them to die, an amount up to the exemption amount would go into a "taxable" trust for the benefit of the surviving spouse. That trust was irrevocable and had restrictions on it. Since no more than the exemption amount went into that trust, no tax was due. Any excess in the deceased spouse's estate went into a different kind of trust for the benefit of the surviving spouse. That trust was eligible for the marital deduction and would be included in the estate of the second spouse to die. In this way, clients could basically shelter up to twice the amount of the exemption from taxes.

For tax purposes, the plan worked well, but for other purposes, it was kind of clumsy. You had to separately fund two trusts and on a somewhat regular basis reallocate assets between them to keep both below the exemption amount. And on the death of the first to die, the survivor had to maintain an irrevocable trust, which could be kind of tricky. If you don't need the tax savings, this is just kind of a clumsy administrative mess. And it can be even worse than that.

I recently got a call from an accountant regarding an estate plan gone bad. He'd represented a married couple. They had a fairly sizable estate. They had worked with an out-of-state attorney to create a joint trust. The trust provided that on the death of the first of them to die, everything went into an irrevocable trust. The survivor was entitled to income and principal on a need basis, but the capital gains that were left in the trust would be taxed at the maximum rate. High taxes; loss of control; bad result.

These older trusts provided that on the death of the first spouse to die, the assets in his or her trust would go into an irrevocable trust. That trust would distribute income, principal on the basis of need, and up to 5% of the principal on demand. These trusts required separate tax returns and would tax capital gains at the maximum rate because of the collapsed tax rates for trusts.

For many clients, these old trusts really don't work as well as they used to, as the case I mentioned above illustrates. When the tax law changed, I sent a notice to clients suggesting that they come in to revise their plans. Not many did. I know there are a lot of these old trusts still out there. Sadly, we will have to deal with this issue more and more as time goes on.

REAL FAMILIES, REAL LIFE

Growing up in the 60s, I had sort of an idyllic idea of family life, learned from the TV shows. We watched, for instance, *Leave It To Beaver*. June was the perfect mom who was always impeccably dressed, calm, and beautiful. Ward never seemed to work that hard but was able to provide a nice home, furnishings, and cars. Wally was Beaver's model brother. And of course, there was Beaver, who was always getting in trouble, but it was always sophomoric high jinks; nothing really dark and sinister. The sinister dimension was covered by Eddie Haskell, but even he was kind of innocent. All of the problems were relatively minor and were resolved in the course of a single episode.

Almost all of the family shows followed the same pattern: *The Andy Griffith Show; The Brady Brunch* (I never did watch that show); *My Three Sons;* and even *Bonanza*. It was a great formula, but it wasn't real.

As enjoyable as these shows were, they didn't then, and they don't now, present a real picture of actual family life. Families are complicated because there are people involved, and people are complicated. Most all of us want to be "normal," but I'm not even sure what that means anymore.

From birth, people have different personalities... sometimes drastically so. Childhood traumas (for instance, the death of a close family member) can mold a person in many ways. And then there are the actual psychological and emotional conditions that can develop apparently for no reason at all. All of these things make life much more challenging.

Sometimes these emotional and psychological conditions can be debilitating. Many times in estate planning, we deal with these situations by creating "special needs trusts." These are trusts that provide the beneficiaries with extra benefits that will not jeopardize state aid. But that may not be the total answer. I'll talk more about these trusts in the next section.

Here I want to talk about situations like George's in our story of Jack and Judy. And George's story is not unique. We have recently run into a number of families with adult children who lived at home and for one reason or another were unable to live on their own. When mom and dad died, they were still in the house and without any real options. Family members had to step in, have a brother or sister declared incompetent, and have them put in some sort of a facility. Hopefully family members will be supportive, but that doesn't always happen.

There is not a single, simple answer to these kinds of problems. If a disability is too severe, then maybe some sort of group home is necessary, such as with George. Someone should be ready to jump in and assume guardianship of the person and custodianship of the assets. If the disability is mild, then maybe he or she can live independently with minimal supervision. But all of that needs to be planned out upfront so that the ball doesn't just get dropped.

And then there's the question of the child's inheritance. In George's case, everything ended up in a conservatorship and was used to provide basic housing. As we discussed earlier, that probably is not a great result. If things are left to him or her outright, will people take advantage of them? Even if it is left in a trust for their benefit, will that jeopardize their state benefits? If it is left in a special needs trust, will that be too restrictive if they don't receive state benefits? If you leave it to another family member, will it actually be used for the benefit of the intended child?

All of these kinds of questions need to be considered. One size does not fit all. It would be a pity to see all of our hard earned assets misapplied due to a lack of planning ... and our most vulnerable children would be the ones who would have to bear the brunt of it.

THE 20 PERCENT

If you watch TV, read magazines or newspapers, or even look at billboards, you get kind of a funny picture of our society. Our media is filled with emaciated, augmented women and men who must spend 8 to 10 hours a day at the gym. And they're all young, healthy, and apparently well-adjusted and happy. We all know that this picture is kind of a cruel parody of life.

As I mentioned, real people are kind of messy. They come in all kinds of shapes and sizes and with different personality types. Although none of us really wants to talk about it, according to the Census Bureau about 20% of the population has special needs of some sort. Those special needs can be emotional, psychological, or physical. And they can vary in intensity from almost imperceptible to crushing. Those needs can be long-lasting or they can be life-threatening. Reportedly about half of those with special needs suffer from a "severe" disability. Life is way more complex than we see in the media.

For parents of children with special needs, this makes life challenging. They may need special medication; they may need special equipment, including chairs and lift, and they may need special care.

Being maybe a little more sensitive to this than many people, I see families heroically struggling to care for their special needs children all the time. It may be special education, therapy, or home modifications. And then there are the daily care needs.

But the scary question is what happens when both (or

either) mom or dad is/are unable to provide that care? What happens when mom and dad are gone? Is there still some way to provide for them?

In planning the estate of people with special needs children, there are several options available, although in my mind only one good one. For instance, you could simply leave that child out of your will or trust. Leave them nothing. After all, they are probably on some government benefit programs. They'll be taken care of, right?

Well, yes and no. The government programs are God-sends for most people in these situations, but they really only provide the minimums. It's kind of spartan, even under the best of circumstances. So that's probably not a great solution.

You could also just leave them their fair share of your estate in trust with the trustee appointed to take care of things. The problem with this option is that these trust funds will in all likelihood be treated as "available funds" for Medicaid purposes, which will be counted in calculating the child's financial need. These funds will probably result in the termination of their state aid until those assets are completely used up.

You could also leave a share of your estate to another child with the understanding (but not the obligation) that they will use the money for the benefit of the special needs sibling. My experience is that this arrangement imposes an awkward burden on the non-disabled child. Also, over time, that money gets mixed up (co-mingled) with the healthy child's other assets. Without meaning to, the money gets absorbed into the person's other assets and becomes indistinguishable. Finally, those funds can be exposed to the non-disabled child's creditors or caught up in a divorce.

In the final analysis, the best option under these circumstances may be a special needs trust (an "SNT"). An SNT is a trust for the benefit of a disabled child. Although such a trust can be set up by the individual (a "self-settled trust") for his or her own benefit, using his or her own assets (such as insurance proceeds from a debilitating accident), that is not what I am talking about here.

This is a "third-party SNT". The statute approving third-party SNTs specifically refers to trusts established by parents, grandparents, or guardians, so it is clear those trusts are acceptable. However, courts in most states have recognized the rights of siblings, friends, or caregivers to establish these trusts as well.

The trustee of such a trust generally cannot provide for housing or food (there are exceptions though). However, the trustee can clearly provide for the disabled child's care by family members; medical services and equipment not covered by government programs; housekeeping, grooming, and meal preparation; certain household costs; certain computer and communication equipment; televisions and tablets; home decoration; vehicles or other transportation; vacations and travel costs; and the list goes on.

One of the drawbacks of a self-settled SNT is that on the beneficiary's death, the trust will probably have to repay the government for any amounts the beneficiary received before making any distributions to family members. Not so with the third-party SNT. With a properly drafted trust, there is no reimbursement obligation. The remaining trust assets can go to the surviving family members.

In the end, families with special needs children should seriously consider an estate plan with an SNT. We don't know what the future holds, but we can assume that government benefits will provide at least a basic safety net. However, as parents, we typically want to provide a little something extra for our children. We can do that with an SNT.

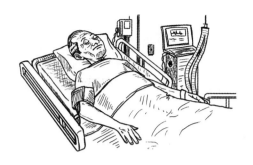

MEDICAID PLANNING

It seems today that a lot of time and energy is being spent trying to get the government to pay for our long-term care. This is not a new thing. I've been practicing law for over 30 years, and I remember doing "Medicaid trusts" when I first started practicing law. Back then, you just had to transfer your assets into a trust, name someone else as the trustee, and leave everything up to the trustee. So simple.

Congress caught on, though. They disagreed with the idea that the government should pay for everyone's nursing home costs, so we started seeing various changes in the law. One of the first changes was to make it a criminal offense to transfer assets to someone else in order to qualify for Medicaid. Some advisors (only jokingly, I think) looked at this as the "grandma goes to prison" plan. Minimum-security prisons (and grandma isn't a real flight risk) aren't really that bad, they reasoned. They provide decent medical care. So grandma will get to go to one of those country club prisons and be taken care of. Congress decided to rethink this plan.

Next, Congress passed a law that said that it was criminal for anyone to assist grandma in transferring assets to someone else in order to qualify for Medicaid. Attorneys, CPAs, and other financial planners understandably reacted badly to this. The concern was that even a legitimate transaction could land you in jail. The professionals raised a hue and cry, and Congress changed the law again.

What we ended up with is the current regimen. Everyone at 65 is eligible for Medicare. It is not a need-based program. However, Medicare only pays for 100 days of rehabilitation care in a nursing facility. It does not pay for long-term nursing care.

Medicaid pays for long-term nursing care. However, Medicaid rules are terribly confusing. The US Supreme Court once referred to the Medicaid rules as a "Byzantine construction... almost unintelligible to the uninitiated."

Those are pretty harsh words from the Supreme Court, but I think I agree. In my career I have done a lot of tax law. I can say that the Medicaid rules make tax law look fairly simple. However, without getting into the deep thicket of Medicaid details, I think we can break Medicaid down into two general categories.

When most people think of Medicaid, we think of the program implemented to assist financially distressed individuals to pay for their medical needs. It covers a limited number of treatments. In order to qualify, the applicant has to be financially needy in one of two ways.

The first classification of qualified applicants is those individuals who are "categorically needy." People are "categorically needy" when they have less than a certain amount of "countable assets." In addition, they cannot have monthly income equal to or greater than a certain amount. Individuals who fall into this category are the people we would typically think of as Medicaid qualified. These amounts can vary somewhat from state to state, and they are periodically adjusted, so you need to check local, current publications.

There is, however, a second class of Medicaid beneficiaries. These individuals are referred to as "medically needy." Qualified applicants still need to have less than a maximum amount of countable assets. However, with regard to income, "medically needy" individuals simply must not have enough income to cover their qualified medical expenses. For instance, if the cost for a person in a nursing home is $6,000 per month and he or she only earns $3,000 per month, Medicaid can make up the difference. That person would fall into the "medically needy" category.

In both of the classifications, there is a limitation on what are "countable assets." Countable assets are any assets an applicant owns (or owned during the five years immediately preceding the application for Medicaid benefits where the assets were not exchanged for something of value – that is, gifts), but it excludes certain assets. For instance, a person's house is not included in "countable assets" for qualification purposes, but the State will put a lien against the house for any Medicaid benefits paid. When the house is sold after the recipient's death, then the State will collect any Medicaid amounts it paid out of the sales proceeds. So the exclusion of the house from countable assets is only temporary.

And then there is the issue of gifting. It seemed to be a simple solution to just give the kids all of your assets right before you went into the nursing home, then the government could pay.

But no matter what you think of Congress, they are not a bunch of dummies. Congress passed a law that provides that beginning in 2006, when an individual applies for Medicaid, he or she has to add back to the countable assets total the value of any assets transferred for less than fair market value during the immediately preceding five-year period (the "look back."). If an asset was transferred for less than fair market value during the look back period, then the government calculates a penalty by dividing the value of the gift by a Medicaid factor. This calculation determines the number of months that the applicant will be disqualified. The disqualification basically runs from the date when the value of the applicant's countable assets drops below the maximum permitted amount. It turns out that the disqualification can run for longer than five years. Timing an application is critical!

Yes, there are some things some people can do. These include long-term care insurance, annuities, and irrevocable trusts. I don't think these are as broad-based as some would have you believe. I would think the best solution would be for the family to take care of mom and dad for as long as it is reasonable to cut down on the costs, but more importantly, to give them the love and attention they deserve, regardless of what might have happened before. However, in the end, there may come a time when a client needs to plan for nursing home costs. That's when some of these techniques will come in handy.

NON-JUDICIAL SETTLEMENT AGREEMENTS

I got a call from a client the other day. It was about her father … well, sort of.

Years ago her father wrote a trust. It provided that on his death, his trustee was to pay off his debts (that's inescapable) and then split his estate between his children in equal shares. Each share was to go in trust to the child. If one of the children died, then his or her share was supposed to go in trust to his or her children.

When he wrote the trust, life was great. His kids were healthy, happily married, and gainfully employed. What could go wrong?

Things happen though. After dad died, one of my client's brothers died. His share went to his son in trust, and my client was the trustee. But she was getting older, and she had health problems. The successor trustee was the nephew's mother, the client's sister-in-law.

I didn't find out the details, but at some point, the sister-in-law kind of went off the tracks. She had developed a drug problem (all too common nowadays). It was pretty serious. She was resorting to some pretty sad means to support her habit.

Her son was living with an uncle. Because of a positive drug test, the mom's baby # 5 had been taken at birth by the state. So sad. She was in pretty desperate straits and in no condition to be in charge of someone else's money. The concern, of course, was that if the mother became trustee of her son's trusts, some or all of the trust assets would be used to support the mother's drug habit.

I told my client that things weren't as hopeless as she might have thought. Under certain circumstances, the law allows "interested persons" to amend a trust even after the grantor has died.

The amendment cannot be contrary to the grantor's original intent. In addition, it has to be something a court could allow. For instance, you can clear up unclear provisions; you can change the authority of the trustee; you can appoint new trustees; or you can approve certain activities of a trustee.

The problem my client had was that in order to change the trustee, the drug-addicted daughter/mother/sister-in-law had to sign off on the agreement as the parent/guardian of the minor grandson. We could get all the other "interested persons" to sign off, but we weren't sure about the mother.

It turned out that with very little resistance she agreed. I think she understood that this money was for her son's college. Her maternal instincts won out. She let the uncle become the successor trustee.

This agreement is what's called a "non judicial settlement agreement." It is permitted by the law to fix relatively minor, undisputed sorts of things. They can be pretty useful when life gets in the way of planning. They can't fix everything, but it's better (and much less expensive) than going to court. There are times when you can't avoid court, but it's probably best to try to minimize that sort of thing.

In the end, we were able to protect the trust assets from the mother's addiction. I'm sure the young man has a lot of pain and sorrow to deal with because of his father's death and his mother's condition. I hope he'll remember that at least this one time, she thought of him first.

ADDICTED BENEFICIARIES

One of the problems we have unfortunately been running into more and more in the past few years is the case of the addicted beneficiary. A child or grandchild who could inherit a large sum of money is struggling with some form of addiction, be it heroin, alcohol, or prescription painkillers. The concern is that giving them unfettered access to large sums of money could ruin them . . . if not kill them. Even if they are off the drugs now, recovery is a daily struggle that never goes away. I greatly admire recovering alcoholics and drug addicts. So the question is, how do you treat them under the estate plan?

One option is to write them out of the estate plan completely and maybe hope that his or her siblings will help them out. That's kind of harsh for one thing. Also, the parent is basically punting the problem to the children. I hate to put that kind of divisive issue between children. I always hope that after mom and dad are gone, the kids will still stay in touch (assuming they stay in touch now). I wouldn't want to create some sort of an additional impediment to those relationships.

Another option is to create a discretionary trust for the addicted heir and have an independent trustee administer it. You can include in the trust a requirement that before the trustee can make any distributions, the beneficiary must, within maybe two weeks of the distribution, take a drug test administered by an independent lab that comes up negative. You could also take it a step further and require the beneficiary to prove how he or she spent any previous distributions. This is possible, but it is fairly labor intensive.

In any event, under these circumstances, careful consideration must be given to protecting the heir from himself or herself. A big inheritance can ruin if not kill a child.

WHEN IS IT THE RIGHT TIME?

Some time ago, an older couple came into my office to do their estate planning. She was 85, and he was 86.

As with all of my clients, I had sent them an estate planning questionnaire that helps me to gather information I'll need to make a recommendation on a plan that would work for them. It asks for family information, financial information, and the names of the people they would want to take care of things when they are no longer able to do things for themselves due to either disability or death.

Right in the middle of the questionnaire is a page that is mainly blank. It asks the client to tell me what they want to have happen to their property upon their death. They can write it out; they can do a diagram; they can draw pictures, whatever. Based on that, I develop a plan.

When I was meeting with this older couple, they had brought in their questionnaire. They had completed the family information. The financial information was pretty detailed and told me what I needed to know. They also had listed the people they wanted to handle things when they couldn't. However, they had left the center page completely blank. This was kind of odd.

So I asked, "What do you want to have happen to your property when you're gone?" And the wife burst into tears.

I don't mean that she just started weeping. It was kind of like wailing.

I was really surprised. I had never had a client do that before (or since, actually). So I turned to the husband and said, "I'm sorry. What did I say?" He leaned forward a little and in a very gravelly voice, he said, "Aw, don't worry. She just doesn't want to admit we're gonna die." Talk about denial. Now to her credit, the only time she had even been in a hospital was when her two boys had been born, but still.

People often tell me that they are going to come see me to get a will or a trust done. My standard response is, "OK, but just don't die in the meantime." I know it's a little insensitive, but it is the hard truth.

I once had a couple whose accountant told them they needed to do their estate planning. They had a pretty good business, a somewhat large family, and some (but not all) of the kids active in the business. We kept trying to get them to come in, but they were always so busy.

One day the accountant called. The husband had died. It was unexpected; a sudden heart attack. The accountant said he would talk to the wife. A few weeks later he called again. She did not want to meet until after the husband's estate and estate tax plan was a little settled.

Time passed. Almost a year later she called. We set an appointment a month or so out for a Monday morning when her kids could join us. The Saturday night before our meeting, the phone rang, and it was one of the sons. His mother had had a massive stroke. She was in the hospital, and although they thought her mind was still there, she could only move her left hand a little. No other movement, not even opening her eyes.

The good news is that mom recovered, but that was pretty close. Although her family was close and supportive, money can make people crazy. And if it's your job, it's even worse.

Nobody wants to think about death, much less their own. It's hard to comprehend for one thing: one minute you're here, and the next, you're gone. It can be pretty depressing.

However, not planning seems kind of irresponsible to me. As I've mentioned, if you have minor children, you don't want them to end up in foster care or have your life insurance be administered by the probate court. You don't want your estate to be probated, generally. I would think you want to be able to name the person who is going to take care of your minor children and administer your assets.

So when is the best time to plan your estate? Honestly, it's right before you die. But no one knows when that day will come, except maybe when it's already upon you. We all know people who have died suddenly from a heart attack or some freak accident. We know other people who were struck with a debilitating disease in the prime of life. We never know when our time will come.

So when is the right time to plan your estate? Now. Don't wait until it's too late.

THE REST OF
THE STORY

As you recall, I started this book with the story of Jack and Judy. I ended that story with a complete catastrophe. However, I said that we would return to it, and here we are.

THE REST OF THE STORY

Judy wakes up like a bomb went off under her. She sits straight upright in bed like a rocket going off. It turns out it was all just a very bad dream.

She turns to Jack, (who did not die) lying peacefully next to her, and yells, "We have to do our estate planning!"

In the morning, they call and make an appointment with an estate planning attorney who publishes a column in the local paper. To prepare for the meeting, he sends them a questionnaire. The questionnaire asks about their family, their assets, what they want to have happen to their property on their deaths, and who they want to handle things.

When they meet with the attorney, they go over the questionnaire together. Based on the information they give to the attorney, he recommends a durable power of attorney to allow someone to handle their financial matters when they become incompetent. He also recommends a medical directive, so someone can make medical decisions when they can't, and also to state their wishes for treatment at the end of their lives. He then recommends a trust to avoid probate and a pour-over will as a safety net. He explains the payment terms and the procedure. He explains that if they decide to do nothing, they owe him nothing at that time. They only owe money if they decide to move forward.

After her nightmare, Judy acted quickly. Without hesitation, she got out her checkbook and made the initial payment. The attorney got drafts of the documents out in a week or so, and a couple of weeks later, they got together to sign the documents.

They signed a deed to transfer their house into the trust and assigned their personal property into the trust. The attorney gave them a detailed letter about retitling bank accounts and investments into their names as trustees and also about changing the beneficiaries of their life insurance and retirement assets. Judy got right on those things.

In the end, Jack and Judy drove off, happy, and that night, Judy slept like Sleeping Beauty.

I always like a happy ending.

POSTSCRIPT

THE YOGI BEAR SYNDROME

One of my favorite cartoon characters is Yogi Bear. For those of you who don't know Yogi, he lived in Jellystone Park. He was always trying to outsmart "Mr. Ranger" with some elaborate scheme to steal "pic-a-nic" baskets. When he hatched a plan, he would always proclaim that he was "smarter than the average bear!" His schemes would inevitably fail, and his side-kick, Boo-Boo, would come to the rescue and make everything alright. Yogi never seemed to have realized that he was the problem and that Boo-Boo was the solution.

I think that all of us suffer more or less from what I call the "Yogi Bear Syndrome." We all think that we are "smarter than the average bear." It's kind of like Garrison Keillor's Lake Wobegon, where "all of the children are above average." We can't all be above average in everything – maybe in some things, but not in everything.

For instance, from the leaks I have caused around my house, I have to admit that I am a below average plumber. I call the professional now. Since electricity can kill you, I don't do anything with electricity more than just replace bulbs and receptacles. With the computerization of cars, they are a complete mystery to me. To quote Dirty Harry, "A man's gotta know his limitations."

So what does all of this have to do with the law? With the advent of the Internet and websites like Rocket Lawyer and Legal Zoom (or as one attorney refers to them, "Rocket Liar" and "Legal Doom"), more and more people are doing their own legal work. You can go online and find a resource for a will, a trust, and any number of corporate documents. You can form your own corporation or limited liability company by just filling in some blanks on a form on the Secretary of State's website. Many times, people don't understand that what they do on the Internet is just the first step. For instance, if all you do is file LLC articles of organization with the Secretary of State, you have not "organized" the LLC. I don't think an LLC without a properly prepared operating agreement is going to protect the member's assets. As a trust officer once said, homemade estate plans are "grocery futures for attorneys." Lots of lawsuits to come.

Believe it or not, lawyers probably know something that you don't know. After excelling in college, they went to law school to learn the basics of the law. After practicing several years, they have some practical experience that non-lawyers don't have. The knowledge and experience does in fact have value. And that value can be invaluable to you.

As much as we hate to admit it, we are probably not smarter than the average bear in everything. We probably are in some things, but certainly not everything. We all need to recognize our limitations.

Avoid the Yogi Bear Syndrome. Call a lawyer when you do your estate plan.

A WORD ABOUT CONFIDENTIALITY

Whatever you tell the lawyer about your case is always confidential. We are prohibited from talking about anything related to the representation of a client. This duty not only applies to current clients, but also to former clients. And former clients include clients who have died.

There are exceptions. For instance, a lawyer can reveal confidential information when ordered to do so by a court. In addition, a lawyer can reveal such information to prevent death or severe bodily injury. Finally, a lawyer can disclose this kind of information about a representation when authorized to do so by the client.

The purpose of this confidentiality is to foster trust between the client and the attorney so that clients are comfortable sharing information with the attorney so the attorney can effectively represent the client. Lawyers are allowed to use hypothetical situations to convey a legal point, provided that "there is no reasonable likelihood that the listener [or reader in our case] will be able to ascertain the identity of the client or the situation involved."

In the course of this book, I have told a number of stories about clients. In each case where the story involves some aspect of the representation of the client, I have obtained the client's consent. In all of my engagement letters, I ask clients whether I can use non-identifiable information about their case to help educate other people about legal issues through my articles, newsletters, and other publications. Where the client has died, I get consent from their personal representatives.

Most of the stories are actually pretty generic and could apply to many clients. In those cases, I have tweaked the facts so that no single client is discussed. When a story is more specific, even if the information does not identify a particular client, I have obtained that client's specific consent to the actual written piece. In addition, some stories do not originate from client representation but come from non-confidential conversations.

So even though this book includes a number of stories about clients, I have respected each client's confidentiality. In that regard, I would like to thank those clients who have consented to my use of their stories, since I believe that stories are the best way to communicate ideas to people. I hope that my readers appreciate this.